RELIGION OF LOVE

RELIGION OF LOVE

BY THE

SWAMI VIVEKANANDA

GYAN

Published by

GYAN

Gyan Publishing House
5, Ansari Road
Daryaganj, New Delhi-110002
Phone: 011-47034999, 9811692060
E-mail: books@gyanbooks.com

Distribution Network
gyanbooks.com
India, USA, Canada, UK, Australia

ISBN: 978-93-6780-540-4 (HB)

First Published, 1907

2nd Impression 2024

Printed at: Gyan Press, Delhi.

RELIGION OF LOVE
Author: SWAMI VIVEKANANDA

RELIGION OF LOVE

BY THE

SWAMI VIVEKANANDA

1907

Swami Vivekananda.

Mohila Press.

RELIGION OF LOVE.

CHAPTER I.

THE best definition given of Bhakti Yoga, is perhaps "that love which the non-discriminating have for the fleeting objects of the senses, the same sort of love men ought to have for Thee, that pleasure in Thee may not vanish from their hearts." We see what a strong love men, who do not know any better, have for sense objects, for money, dress, for their wives and children and friends, and possessions, what a tremendous clinging they have to all these things. So with this definition the sage says, "I will have that attachment, that tremendous clinging, only for Thee." This love when given to God is called *Bhakti*. *Bhakti* is not destructive; it teaches us that no one of the faculties we have has been given in vain, that through them is the natural way to come to liberation. *Bhakti* does not restrain anything, it does not go against nature, only gives it a higher and more powerful direction. How naturally we love objects of the senses, and we cannot but do so, because they are so real to us. We do not see anything real about higher things ordinarily, but when a man has seen something real beyond these senses, beyond the universe of senses, the idea is that you should let the same attachment be, only transfer it to this object beyond the senses, which is God. And when the same kind of love that has been before given to sense objects, is given to God, it is called *Bhakti*. According to the sage, Ramanuja, these are the preparations for getting that intense love.

The first is *viveka,* and it is a very curious thing, especially to people of the West. It means, according to Ramanuja, "discrimination of food." Food contains all the energies that go to make up the forces of our body and mind; all that I am now was in the bit of food that I ate; it has been transferred, and conserved, and given new directions in my body, but my body and mind have nothing essentially different from the food that I ate. Just as in the material world we find force and matter, and this force and matter in us become body and mind, so, essentially, the difference between body and mind and the food we eat is only in manifestation. It being so, that out of the material particles of our food we construct the instrument of thought, and that from the finer forces lodged in these particles we manufacture thought itself, it naturally follows, that both this thought and the instrument will feel the effect of the food we take. There are certain kinds of food that produce a certain change in the mind; we see it obviously every day. There are other sorts which produce a change in the body, and in the long run have a tremendous effect on the mind. It is a great thing to learn; a good deal of the misery we are suffering is simply occasioned by the food we take. You find that after a heavy and indigestible meal it is very hard to control the mind; it is running, running all the time. Then there are certain foods which are exciting; if you eat such food, also, you find that you cannot control the mind. It is obvious that after drinking a large quantity of wine, or some other alcoholic beverage, a man finds that his mind is not to be controlled; it runs away from his control. According to Ramanuja there are three things in food we must avoid. First, *jati*, the nature, or species, of the food; all exciting food should be avoided, as meat, for instance; this should be avoided because it is by its very nature impure. We can only get it by taking the life of another. We get pleasure for a moment, and another creature has to give up its life to give us that pleasure. Not only so, but we demoralise other human beings. It would be rather better if every man who eats meat killed the animal himself, but, instead of doing that, society gets a class of persons to do that business for them, and for doing so society hates them. I do not know the law here, but in England no butcher can serve on a jury, the idea being that he is cruel by nature. Who makes them cruel? Society. If we did not eat beef and mutton they would not be butchers. Eating meat is only allowable to people who do very hard work, and who are not going to be Bhaktas, but if you are going to be Bhaktas, meat should be avoided. Also, all exciting foods, such as onions, garlic, and all evil-smelling food, as "sauerkraut." Any food that has been standing for days, and is almost rotten, any food whose natural juices have been almost dried up, any food that is malodorous should be avoided.

The next thing as regards food is still more intricate to Western minds—what is called *âsraya* (lit., the person or thing in which any particular quality is present), the person from whom it comes. This is rather a mysterious theory of the Hindus. The idea is that each man has a certain aura round him, and whatever he touches, a part of his character, as it were, his influence, is left on that thing. Just as effluvia is coming out of each man's body, so character is coming out of him, and whatever he touches takes it. So we must take care who touches our food when it is cooked, any wicked or immoral person must not touch it. One who wants to be a Bhakta must not sit down with people whom he knows to be very wicked, because that infection will come through the food. The other is *nimitta.* It is very easy. Dirt and dust and all these things must not be in food. Food should not be brought from the market and placed on the table unwashed, with the dirt and dust of thirty-three States of the Union on it. We must also cease to have anything to do with spittle. God has given plenty of water to wash things with. and this tremendous habit of touching the lips and touching everything with spittle is the most horrible thing I have seen. The mucous membrane is the most delicate part of the body, and all tendencies are conveyed very easily by the spittle. So touching the lips with the fingers, when the food has to be put into the mouth with them is very dangerous. Then we must not eat food half of which has been eaten by someone else ; one man takes a bite of an apple and gives it to another to eat. When these things are avoided in food, the food becomes pure ; pure food brings a pure mind, and a pure mind is a constant memory of God.

Let me tell you the same thing as explained by another commentator. He says when food is pure the mind becomes pure, when the mind is pure the memory of God becomes constant. Sankaracharya takes quite another view. This word for food, in the Sanskrit is derived from the word to gather ; gathered in. What is his explanation ? He says when food is pure the mind will become pure, really means that in regard to becoming attached to the senses we should avoid these things. First as to attachment ; we must not be extremely attached to anything excepting God. See everything, do everything, touch everything, but be not attached. As soon as that extreme attachment comes a man loses himself, he is no more master of himself, he is a slave. If a woman is tremendously attached to a man she becomes a slave to that man, or the man to the woman. There is no use in being a slave. There are higher things in this world than becoming a slave to a human being. Love and do good to everybody, but do not become a slave. In the first place it degenerates us, individually, and in the second place makes us extremely selfish. From this failing we want to injure others to do good to those we love. A good many of the wicked deeds done in this world are really done through attachment to certain persons. So all attachment of this kind should be avoided, barring attachment to good works, but love should be given to everybody.

There should be no jealousy in regard to objects of the senses ; jealousy is the root of all evil, and a most difficult thing to conquer. We are becoming jealous every moment of our lives ; we have no other motives. Delusion. We are always taking one thing for another, and acting upon that, and the result is we bring misery upon ourselves. We are taking the bad for the good. Anything that titillates our nerves for a moment we think the highest good, and we plunge into it immediately and find it gives us a tremendous blow, but too late. Every day we are running into this error, and we often continue it all our lives. All sorts of things we engage in, thinking they will be very good, because they please the senses for a moment, and, when too late, we find our mistake. When the senses, without being extremely attached, and without jealousy, or without delusions, work in the world, this is called food, according to Sankaracharya. When the food is purified, is when the mind is able to take in objects and think about them without attachment, jealousy and delusion ; then the mind becomes pure, and when that is the case, constant memory of God is in that mind.

It is quite natural that all of you should say, "that is the best meaning after all," but there is this addition, that you must not neglect the first. It is only when you take care of that, the real material food, that the rest will come. It is a very true thing that mind is the master, but very few of us are not bound by the senses. Who of you here could drink a bottle of whiskey and stand without reeling ? I do not think anyone. That shows we are all controlled by matter, and as long as we are controlled by matter we must take material aids, and then, when we have become strong we can eat anything we like. We have to follow Ramanuja, and take care of food and drink, but at the same time we must take care of our mental food. It is very easy to take care in our material food ; but mental work must go along with it ; then gradually our spiritual self will become stronger and stronger, and the physical self will then fall down by itself. Then will come the time when you will find that no food hurts you, that no amount of dyspepsia will be able to throw you off your balance. Any little trouble in your liver now makes you mad. The great danger is that every man wants to jump at the highest ideal, but jumping is not the way ; we only break our legs and fall down. We are bound down here, and we have to slowly break our chains. This is called *viveka*, discrimination of food. The next is called *vimoksha*, freedom, he who wants to love God must get rid of extreme desires ; desire nothing except God. This world is good so far as it helps one to go to the higher world. The objects of the senses are good so far as they help us to attain higher objects. We always forget that this world is a means to an end, and not the end itself. If this were the end we would be immortal here in our physical body; we would never die. But we see people every moment dying around us, and yet, foolishly, we think we will never die, and from that conviction we come to think that this life is the goal. That is the case with ninty-nine per cent. of us. This should be given up at once. This world is good so far as it is a means to perfect ourselves, and as soon as it has ceased to do that it is evil, nothing but evil. So wife, children, husband, money, dollars, or learning, are good, so long as they help us forward; but as soon as they have ceased to do that they are nothing but evil. If the wife help us to God, that is a good wife. So with husbands and children, or if money helps a man to do good to others, it is something real; but if not, it is simply a mass of evil, and the sooner we throw it out the better.

The next is *abhyâsa*, practice. Mind should always go towards God, no other things have any right to enter our minds. It should always continuously think of God, but it is a very hard task, yet it can be done by persistent practice. What we are now is the result of past practice. Practice makes us what we will be. So practice the other way; one sort of turning round has brought us this way, turn the other way and get out of it as soon as you can. Thinking of the senses has brought us down here to live a moment, to cry one moment, to rejoice the next moment, to be at the mercy of every breeze, slave to a word, to a bit of food. This is a shameful thing, and yet we call ourselves spirits, and all those high words which mean nothing to us. We are slaves of the world, and we have brought ourselves to this by going towards the senses. Go the other way, think of God; let the mind not think of any physical or mental enjoyment, but of God alone. When it tries to think of anything else, give it a good blow, so that it may turn round and think of God. "As oil poured from one vessel to another falls in an unbroken line as the chimes come from a distance and their sounds fall upon the ear in one continuous stream, so will this mind come towards God in one continuous stream." We should not only have this practice for the mind, but the senses should be employed. Instead of hearing foolish things we must hear God; instead of talking foolish things we must talk of God. Instead of reading foolish books we must read good books, which tell of God.

The greatest aid to this practice of keeping God in memory is, perhaps, sound. Music. It is said by Narada, the great teacher of *Bhakti*, "I do not live in heaven, nor do I live in the heart of the Yogi, but where my brothers sing my praise, there am I." Music has such tremendous power over the human mind ; it brings it to concentration in a moment. You will find the dull, ignorant, low, brute-like human beings, who can never make their minds steady for a moment, when they hear attractive music, immediately become charmed. Even the minds of animals, dogs and lions, and cats and serpents, become charmed with music.

The next is *kriyà*, work. Doing good to others. That memory of God will not come to the selfish man. The more we come out and do good to others, the more our hearts will be purified, and God will be in them. According to our scriptures, there are five works, called five worships. First, study. A man must study every day something holy and something good. Second, worship of God, or angels, or saints, as it may be. Third, our duty to our forefathers. Fourth, our duty to human beings. Man has no right to live in a house himself, until he builds for the poor also, or for anybody who needs it. The householder's house should be open to everybody that is poor and suffering ; then he is a real householder. If he builds a house only for himself and his wife to enjoy, then they are the only two persons in the world, and he will never be a lover of God. It would be a most selfish act. No man has the right to cook food for himself; it is for others, and he should have what remains. It is a common thing in India that when different things come into the market, as strawberries, or mangoes, a man buys so much of them and gives to the poor. Then he eats, after doing that, and it is a very good example to follow in this country. This training will make a man unselfish, and on the other hand, will be a constant training to wife and children. The Hebrews in olden times used to give the first fruits to God, but they do not now, I am afraid. The first of everything should go to the poor: we have only a right to what remains. The poor are God's representatives; anyone that suffers is His representative. Without giving, that man who eats, and enjoys eating, is enjoying sin. Fifth, our duty to lower animals. It is diabolical to say that all these animals are created for men, to be killed and used in any way man likes. It is the devil's gospel, not God's. Think what a diabolical thing it is that we should take them and cut them up to see whether a nerve quivers or not in a certain part of the body. The time will come when that man will be amenable to the penal code of every country. I am glad that in our country such things are not countenanced by Hindus, whatever encouragement they may get from the foreign government we are under. One portion of the food belongs to the animals also. They should be given food every day; there ought to be hospitals in every city in this country for poor, lame, or blind horses, cats, dogs and cows, and they should be fed and taken care of.

Then there are *kalyâna*, beauty, purity, *satyam*, truthfulness. He who is true, unto him the God of truth comes. Thought, word, and deed should be perfectly true. Next *ârjavam*, straightforwardness, rectitude. The word means to be simple, no crookedness in the heart, no double dealing. Even if it is a little harsh, go straight forward and not crooked. *Dayâ*, pity, compassion. *Dânam*, charity. *Ahimsa*, not injuring any being by thought, word, or deed. There is no higher virtue than charity. The lowest man is he whose hand is towards himself and takes, and the highest man whose hand is out and gives. The hand was made for that, to give always. Give the last bit of bread you have, even if you are starving. You will be free in a moment, if you starve yourself to death by giving to another. Immeditately you will become perfect you will become God. People who have children hanging on to them are bound already. They cannot give away. They want to enjoy children, and they must pay for it. Are there not enough children in the world? It is only selfishness which says, "I'll have a child for myself." *Anavasada* (lit., not sitting down, not desponding), cheerfulness, Despondency is not religion, whatever else it may be. By pleasing always, smiling, it takes you nearer to God, nearer than any prayer. How can a mind that is gloomy and dull love? If they talk of love it is false; they want to kill others. Think of all these fanatics; they make the longest faces, and all their religion is to go and fight against others in word and act. Think of them in history, and of what they would do now. They would deluge the whole world in blood to-morrow if it would bring them power, because gloomy things are their God. Worshipping that terrible being, and making long faces, they lose every bit of love from their hearts, and they would have no mercy on anybody. So the man who always feels miserable will never come to God. It is not religion, it is diabolism, to say "I am so miserable." Every man has his own burden to bear. If you are miserable, try to be happy, try to conquer it.

God is not to be reached by the weak; never be weak. You must be strong; you have infinite strength within you. How else will you conquer anything? How else will you come to God? At the same time we must avoid excessive merriment, *uddhasa* it is called. A mind in that state never becomes calm ; it becomes fickle. Excessive merriment will always be followed by sorrow. Tears and laughter are near kin. People so often run from one extreme to the other. Let the mind be cheerful, but calm. Never let it run into excesses, because every excess will be followed by a reaction.

These, according to Ramanuja, are the preparations for *Bhakti*.

CHAPTER II.

The philosophers who wrote on *Bhakti* define it as extreme love for God. Why a man should love God is the question to be solved, and until we understand that we will not be able to grasp the subject at all. There are two entirely different ideals of life. All of us in any country who have any religion know that man is a body and a spirit also. But there is a great deal of difference as to the goals of human life. In the western countries, as a rule, people lay more stress on the body aspect of man; those philosophers who wrote on *Bhakti* in India lay stress on the spiritual side of man, and this difference seems to be typical of the oriental and occidental nations. It is so even in common language. In England you say a man gave up his ghost; in India a man gave up his body, when speaking of death. The one idea is that man *is* a body and *has* a soul, the other that man *is* a soul and *has* a body. More intricate problems arise out of this. It naturally follows that that state whose ideal is that man is a body and has a soul lays all the stress on the body. If you ask why man lives, you will be told to enjoy the senses, to feel, to hear, and see, and eat, and drink; to enjoy possessions, and wealth, and father, and mother, and domestic relations, and all these things, and it never goes beyond this. He cannot dream of anything beyond, even if he is told of it ; his idea of a future life would be a continuation of this enjoyment ; he is very sorry that he cannot continue it all the time here, but he has to depart, and he thinks that somehow or other he will go to some place where the same thing will be renewed ; he will have the same enjoyments, the same senses, only heightened and strengthened, and so forth. He wants to worship God, because God is the means to attain this end. The goal of his life is enjoyment of sense objects, and he comes to know there is a Being who can give him a very long lease of these enjoyments, and that is why he worships God. On the other hand the idea is that God is the goal of life ; there is nothing beyond God, and these sense enjoyments are simply something through which we are passing now in the hope of getting better things. Not only so ; it would be disastrous and terrible if man had nothing but these sense enjoyments. In our every day life we find that the less the sense enjoyments the higher the life of that man. Look at the dog ; he is eating ; no man ever ate with the same satisfaction. Look at the pig giving grunts of satisfaction as he eats ; no man was ever born who could eat that way.

Think of the power of hearing in the lower animals, the power of seeing; all the senses are highly developed. Man could never have them. Their enjoyment of the senses is simply extreme; they become simply mad with delight and pleasure, and the lower the man the more delight he finds in the senses. As you get higher the goal becomes reason and love. These faculties are coming and you are losing that power of enjoying the senses. For illustration's sake, if we take for granted that a certain amount of power is given to man, and that that can be either spent on the body, on the mind, or on the spirit; then all the power spent on any one of these leaves just so much less to be expended on the others. The ignorant or savage races, have much finer sensual faculties than the civilised races, and this is, in fact, one of the lessons we learn from history, that as a nation becomes civilised the nerve organisation becomes finer, and they become physically weaker. Civilize a savage race and you will find the same thing; another barbarian race comes up and conquers them. It is nearly always the barbarian race that conquers. We see then that if our desires are only that we shall have nice sense enjoyments all the time, we are desiring an impossible thing, because then we should become brutes. A man does not know what he is asking for when he says he will go to a place where his sense enjoyments will be intensified; that he can have by going down to the brutes. The pig never thinks he is eating something filthy. It is his heaven, and if the greatest archangel came and looked on, the pig would not deign to look at him; his whole existence is in his eating.

So with men; they are like pigs, wallowing in the mire of the senses, and cannot see anything beyond. This sense enjoyment is what they want, and the loss of it is the loss of heaven to them. These can never be Bhaktas in the highest sense of the word; they can never be true lovers of God. At the same time though this lower ideal be followed it will in the course of time change; each man will find that there is something higher, of which he did not know, and so this clinging to life and to things of the senses will gradually die away. When I was a little boy at school I had a fight with another school-fellow about some sweet-meat or other, and he being the stronger boy snatched it from my hand. I remember the feeling I had; I thought that boy was the most wicked boy ever born, and that as soon as I grew strong enough I would punish him; there was no punishment sufficient for his wickedness; he ought to be hanged and quartered. We have both grown up now and we are fast friends. So this world is full of babies to whom eating and drinking, and all these little cakes are everything; the loss of any bit of it is awful for them. They will dream of these cakes, and their idea of future life is where these cakes will be plentiful. Think of the American Indian who believes that his future life will be in a place which is a very good hunting ground. Each one of us has an idea of a heaven just as we want it, but in course of time, as we grow older, and see higher things, we catch higher glimpses beyond all these things; let us not get beyond these in the ordinary way of modern times, by not believing in anything—that is destruction. The agnostic who thus destroys everything is mistaken, the Bhakta sees things higher. The agnostic does not want to go to heaven because he has none, and the son of God does not want to go to heaven because he thinks it child's play. What he wants is God. What can be a higher end than God? God Himself is the highest goal of man; see Him; enjoy Him. We can never conceive anything higher because God is perfection. We cannot conceive of any higher enjoyment than that of love, but this word love has different meanings. It does not mean the ordinary selfish love of the world; it is blasphemy to call that love. This love for our children and our wives is mere animal love; that love which is perfectly unselfish is the only love, and that is through God. It is a very difficult thing to attain to. We are passing through all these different loves, those of loving our children, and father, and mother, and various attachments; we slowly exercise the faculty of love, but in the majority of cases we never learn anything from it, we become bound down to one step, and to one person. In some cases men come out of this bondage. Men are ever running after wives, and wealth, and fame in this world; sometimes they are thumped very hard on the head, and they find out what this world really is. No one in this world can really love anything but God. Man finds out that human love is all hollow. Men cannot love; they talk and talk. The wife says, "I love you husband," and weeps, and kisses him all the time; but as soon as he dies the first thing she thinks about is the bank account, what she shall do the next day. The husband loves the wife, but when she becomes sick, and loses her beauty, or becomes haggard, or makes a mistake, ceases to care for her. All the love of the world is hypocrisy and hollowness.

A finite subject cannot love, nor a finite object be loved. When the object of the love of a human being is dying every moment, and his mind also is constantly changing as his growth proceeds; what eternal love can you expect to find in the world?

There cannot be any love but in God; why then all these loves? These are mere mistakes. There is a power behind impelling us forward towards love; we don't know where to seek for the real object, but this love is sending us forward in search of it. Again and again we find our mistake. We grasp for something, and find it slips through our fingers, and then we grasp for something else. On and on, and then comes light; we come to God; the only one who loves; His love knows no change, is ever ready to take us in. How long would any of you bear me if I injured you? He in whose mind is no anger or hatred or envy, who never loses his balance, or dies, or is born; who is he but God? But it is a very long way to God, and a very difficult one; very few people attain to it. We are all babies struggling. Millions make a trade of religion. Everyone talks of it, but very few attain to it; a few in a century attain to that love of God, and the whole country becomes blessed and hallowed and purified, as when one sun arises all darkness vanishes. When a son of God appears whole tracts become blessed and purified. Few such are born in any one century in the whole world, but we will all make the attempt, and who knows but you may be the next one, or I. Let us struggle, therefore. We say that a wife loves her husband; she thinks that her whole soul is absorbed in him ; a baby comes, and half of it goes out the baby, or more. She herself will feel that the same love of husband does not exist now So with the father. We always find that when more intense objects of love come to us the previous love slowly vanishes. When you were at school you thought that a few of your schoolfellows were the dearest beings that you had in your life, or your father or mother were so ; then came the husband or wife, and immediately the old feeling disappeared, and the new love became intensest. One star arises, another bigger one comes, and then a bigger, and at last the sun comes, and all the lesser lights vanish. That sun is God. All these stars are the smaller loves. When that sun bursts upon him man becomes mad, what Emerson calls "a God-intoxicated man." Man becomes transfigured into God, animals become transfigured, everything is merged in that one ocean of love. Ordinary love is mere animal attraction. Otherwise why should the distinction between the sexes be required ? If one kneels before an Image it is horrible idolatry, but if one kneels before husband or wife it is quite permissible.

These are things through which we have to pass. You have to first clear the ground ; upon your view of life the whole theory of love will rest.

To think that this world is the aim and end of life is simply brutal and degenerating. Any man who starts in life with that idea simply degenerates himself. He will never rise higher ; he will never catch this glimpse from behind, he will be always a slave to the senses. He will struggle for the dollar that will get him a few cakes to eat. Better die than live that life. Slaves of this world, slaves of your senses, rouse yourselves ; there is something higher than this. Do you think this man, this infinite spirit, was born to be a slave to his eyes, his nose and his ears. There is an infinite, omniscient spirit behind that can do everything, break every bond, and that spirit you are, and you get that power through love. So this is the ideal, you must remember. We are not going to get it to-morrow. We may fancy that we have got it, but it would be fancy after all ; it is a long, long way off. We must take the man where he stands, and help him upwards, if it is possible. Man stands in materialism ; you and I are all materialists. Our talking about God, and spirit, are good, but they are simply certain words used in our society ; we have learned them parrot-like and talk them out. So we have to take ourselves where we are as materialists, and must take the help of matter, and so we shall go on slowly, slowly, until we become real spiritualists, feel ourselves spirits, understand the spirit, and find that this world which we call the infinite is but one gross external form of that world which is behind.

But something besides that is necessary. You read in the Sermon on the Mount, "Ask and it shall be given unto you, knock and it shall be opened unto you, seek and you shall find." The difficulty is, who seeks, who wants? We all say we know God. One man writes a huge book to disprove God, another to prove Him. One man thinks it his duty to prove Him all his life, and another to disprove Him, and he goes about to teach man there is no God. What is the use of writing a book either to prove or disprove God? What does it matter to most people whether there is a God or not? The majority of men in this city rise in the morning, and go down to breakfast; God did not come to help him in his dressing, or in his eating. He goes down to work, and works the whole day, and makes money; he puts it in a bank, comes home, eats his dinner and goes to bed, just like a machine, with no thought of God, and feeling no need of Him. He has four eternal duties, eating, drinking, sleeping and continuing the species. Then one day comes Death and says "Get up." The man says, "One minute more, I want a little more time. I want to see my son John get a little bigger." But Death says, "Come at once. Habeas Corpus." So it goes on. So goes poor John; what shall we say to poor John, he never found anything in which God was the highest; perhaps he was a pig in the past, and he is much better as a man. But all the world are not poor Johns, there are some who get a little awakening. Some misery comes, someone whom we love most dies, that thing upon which we had bent our whole soul, that thing for which we had cheated the whole world, perhaps our own brother, for whom we had done everything horrible, perhaps that vanishes, and a blow comes to John. Perhaps a voice comes in his soul and asks, "What after this?" That son to make whom rich John has been cheating everybody and starving himself, perhaps dies, and John is awakened by the blow. That wife to get whom John was like a mad bull, fighting everybody, for whom John was accumulating money to get new dresses and jewellery, one day she dies suddenly, what then? Sometimes death comes without a blow, but there are very few cases. With the majority of us when anything slips through our fingers we say, "What then?" Such a tremendous clinging to the senses do we suffer from! You have heard of a drowning man clutching at a straw; a man will clutch at a straw first, and when it fails he will say some one must help me. Still people must in the English phrase, "sow their wild oats," before they can rise to higher things.

But this *Bhakti* is a religion; religion is not for the many, that is impossible. That sort of knee drill, that standing up and sitting down, may be for the many, but religion is for the few. There are in each country only a few hundreds who can be, and will be religious. The others cannot because they will not be awakened, they do not want. The chief thing is to *Want* God, we want everything except God, because our ordinary interests are supplied by the external world; it is only when our necessities have gone beyond the external world that we want a supply from the internal, from God. So long as our needs are confined within the narrow limits of this physical universe we cannot have any need for God; it is only when we have become satiated with everything here, and want something beyond, that we look beyond for a supply. It is only when the need is there that the demand will come. Have done with this child's play of the world as soon as you can, and then you will feel the necessity of something beyond the world, and the first step in religion will come.

There is a form of religion because it is fashionable; my friend has much furniture in her parlour, it is the fashion to have a Japanese vase, perhaps, so I must have one, even if it costs a thousand dollars. Then I will have a little religion and join a church. *Bhakti* is not for such. That is not "want," want is that without which we cannot live. We want breath, we want food, we want clothes, without them we cannot live. When a man loves a woman in this world there are times when he feels that without her he cannot live, although that is a mistake. When a husband dies the wife thinks for five minutes she cannot live without him, but she lives all the same. I have thought many times when my relatives have died that I would not live ; I loved them very much, but I am alive all the same. This is the secret of necessity, it is that without which we cannot live, either it must come to us or we die. When the time comes that we feel the same about God, or in other words, we want something beyond this world, something above all material forces, then we may become Bhaktas. What are our little lives when, as it were, cloud passes away, for a moment, and we get one glimpse from beyond, and for that moment all these lower desires seem like a drop in the ocean. Then the soul grows, and feels the want of God, and must have Him. For the first step *what* do we want ? Let us ask ourselves this question every day, do we want

God? You may read all the books in the universe, but this love is not to be got by the power of speech, not by the highest intellect, not by the study of various sciences. Whom He desires he will get Love, unto him He desires Himself, Love is always mutual, reflective. You may hate me, and if I begin to love you, you repulse me. In a month or a year, if I persist, you are bound to love me. It is a psychological phenomenon. Whom the Lord loves he loves the Lord, his whole soul clings unto Him. As the loving wife thinks for her departed husband, with the same love which we give to our sons we must desire the Lord, and then we will find God, and all books, and the various sciences would not teach us anything. By reading books we become parrots; no one becomes learned by reading books. If a man reads but one word of love he indeed becomes learned. So we want to first get that desire. Let us ask ourselves each day, do we want God? When we begin to talk religion, and especially when we take a high position and begin to teach others, ask ourselves the same question. I find many times that I don't want God, I want bread more. I may go mad if I don't get a piece of bread; many ladies will go mad if they don't get a diamond pin, but they do not have the same desire for God; they do not know the only Reality that is in the universe.

There is a proverb in our language—If I want to be a hunter I'll hunt the rhinoceros, if I want to be a robber I'll rob the king's treasury. What is the use of robbing beggars or hunting ants? So if you want to love, love God. Who cares for these things of the world? I am rather a plain-spoken man, but I mean well, I want to tell you the truth, I don't want to flatter you, it's not my business. If I had wanted to do that I would have opened a fashionable church in Fifth Avenue. You are like my children, I want to tell you the truth. This world is utterly false, all the great teachers of the world have found that out, there is no way out of it but through God. He is the goal of our life; all ideas that the world is the goal of life are pernicious. This world, this body, have their own value, a secondary value, as a means to an end, but the world should not be the end. Unfortunately too often we make the world the end and God the means. We find people going to church and saying, God give me so-and-so, God heal my disease. They want nice healthy bodies, and because they hear that someone is sitting somewhere who will do this work for them they go and pray to Him. It is better to be an Atheist than to have such an idea of religion. As I have told you this *Bhakti* is the highest ideal; I don't know whether we will reach it or not in millions of years to come, but you must make it your highest ideal, make your senses aim at the highest. If you cannot get to the end you will at least get somewhere. We have slowly to work through the world and the senses to reach God.

CHAPTER III.

Every soul is destined to be perfect, and every being, in the end, will attain to that state. Whatever we are now, is the result of whatever we have been, or thought, in the past, and whatever we will be in the future will be the result of what we do or think now. But this does not preclude our receiving help from outside; the possibilities of the soul are always quickened by some help from outside, so much so, that in the vast majority of cases in the world help from outside is almost absolutely necessary. Quickening influence comes from outside, and that works upon our own potentialities, and then the growth begins, spiritual life comes, and man becomes holy and perfect in the end. This quickening impulse, which comes from outside, cannot, be received from books; the soul can only receive impulse from another soul, and from nothing else. We may study books all our lives, we may become very intellectual, and, in the end, we find we have not developed at all spiritually. It does not follow, that a high order of intellectual development, always shows an equivalent development of the spiritual side of man; on the other hand, we find cases almost every day where the intellect has become very highly developed at the expense of the spirit.

Now, in intellectual development we can get much help from books, but in spiritual development almost nothing. In studying books, sometimes we are deluded into thinking that we are being spiritually helped, but if we analyse ourselves, we will find that only our intellect has been helped and not the spirit. That is the reason why almost every one of us can *speak* most wonderfully on spiritual subjects, but when actions come, we find ourselves so woefully deficient. It is because books cannot give us that impulse from outside. To quicken the spirit that impulse must come from another soul. That soul from which this impulse come is called the Guru, the teacher, and the soul to which the impulse is conveyed is called the disciple, the student. In order to convey this impulse in the first place the soul from which it comes must possess the power of transmitting it, as it were, to another, and in the second place the object to which it is transmitted must be fit to receive it. The seed must be a living seed, and the field must be ready ploughed, and when both these conditions are fulfilled, a wonderful growth of religion takes place. "The speaker of religion must be wonderful, so shall the hearer be," and when both of these are really wonderful, extraordinary, then alone will splendid spiritual growth come, and not otherwise. These are the real teachers, and these are the real students; besides these the others are playing with spirituality; just have a little intellectual struggle, just satisfying a little curiosity, but are standing only on the outward fringe of the horizon of religion. There is some value in that; all comes in course of time, a real thirst for religion may be awakened, and it is a mysterious law of nature, that as soon as the field is ready the seed *must* come, as soon as the soul wants religion, the transmitter of religious force *must* come.

"The seeking sinner meeteth the seeking Saviour." When the power that attracts in the receiving soul is full and ripe, the power which answers to that attraction must come.

But there are great dangers in the way. There is the danger to the receiving soul of mistaking its momentary emotion for real religious yearning. We find that in ourselves, many many times in our lives, somebody dies whom we loved; we receive a blow for a moment; we think that this world is slipping between our fingers, and that we want something higher, and that we are going to be religious. In a few days that wave has passed, and we are left stranded where we were. We ofttimes mistake such impulses for real thirst after religion, but as long as these momentary emotions are thus mistaken, that continuous, real, want of the soul will not come, and we shall not find the "transmitter."

So, when we complain that we have not got the truth, and that we want it so much, instead of complaining, our first duty ought to be to look into our own souls, and find whether we *really* want it; in the vast majority of cases we will find that we are not fit; we do not want; there was no thirst after the spiritual. There are still more difficulties for the "transmitter."

There are many who, though immersed in ignorance, yet, in the pride of their hearts, think they know everything, and not only stop there, but offer to take others on their shoulders, and thus "the blind leading the blind, they both fall into the ditch." The world is full of these; everyone wants to be a teacher, every beggar wants to make a gift of a million dollars. Just as the latter is ridiculous, so are these teachers.

How are we to know a teacher then? In the first place the sun requires no torch to make it visible; we do not light a candle to see the sun; when the sun rises we instinctively become aware of its rising, and when a teacher of men comes to help us, the soul will instinctively know that it has found the truth. Truth stands on its own evidences; it does not require any other testimony to attest it; it is self-effulgent. It penetrates into the inmost corners of our nature, and the whole universe of nature stands up and says "this is truth." These are the very great teachers, but we can get help from the lesser ones also, and we ourselves are not always sufficiently intuitive to be certain of our judgment of the man from whom we receive, so there ought to be certain tests. There are certain conditions necessary from the taught, and also from the teacher. The conditions necessary in the taught are purity, a real thirst after knowledge, perseverance. No impure soul can be religious; that is the one great condition; purity in every way is absolutely necessary. The other condition is a real thirst after knowledge. Who *wants?* That is the question. We get whatever we want—that is an old, old law. He who wants, gets. To want religion is a very difficult thing, not so easy as we generally think. Then we always forget that religion does not consist in hearing talks, or in reading books, but it is a continuous struggle, a grappling with our own nature, a continuous fight, till the victory is achieved. It is not a question of one or two days, of years or of lives, but it may be hundreds of lifetimes, and you must be ready for that. It may come immediately, or it may not come in hundreds of lifetimes, and we must be ready for that. The student who sets out with such a spirit finds success.

In the teacher we must first see that he knows the secret of the scriptures. The whole world reads scriptures, Bibles, Vedas, Qur'ans, and all these, but they are only words, external arrangement, syntax, the etymology, the philology, the dry bones of religion. The teacher may be able to find what is the age of any book, but words are only the external forms in which things come. Those who deal too much in words, and let the mind run always in the force of words, lose the Spirit. So the teacher must be able to know the *spirit* of the scriptures. The network of words is like a huge forest, in which the human mind loses itself and finds no way out. The various methods of joining words, the various methods of speaking a beautiful language, the various methods of explaining the dictions of the scriptures, are only for the enjoyment of the learned; they donot attain perfection; they are simply desirous to show their learning, so that the world may praise them, and see that they are learned men. You will find that no one of the great teachers of the world went into these various explanations of texts; there is no attempt at "text torturing"; no saying "this word means this and this is the philological connection between this and that word." You study all the great teachers the world has produced, and no one of them goes that way. Yet *they* taught; while others, who have nothing to teach, will take up a word and write a three-volume book on that word's origin, the man who used it, and what that man used to eat, and how he used to sleep. My master used to tell a story of a few men who went into a mango orchard, and most of them were busy in counting the leaves, and examining the colour of the leaves, and the size of the twigs, and the number of branches, and so forth, and began to note down everything, and got up a wonderful discussion on each of these, but one of them, more sensible than the others, began to eat the mangoes. So leave this counting leaves and twigs, and note-taking to others; that work has its value in its proper place, but not here, in the spiritual. Those men never become spiritual through such work; you have never once seen a strong spiritual man among these "leaf counters." Religion is the highest aim of man, the highest glory, and it is the easiest, it does not require so much botheration as "leaf-counting." If you want to be a Christian it is not necessary to know where Christ was born, in Jerusalem or Bethlehem, what He was doing, or just the exact date on which He pronounced the Sermon on the Mount; you only require to *feel* the Sermon on the mount. It is not necessary to read 2,000 words on when it was pronounced. All that is for the enjoyment of the learned, let them have it; say amen to that; let *us* "eat the mangoes."

The second condition necessary in the teacher is that he must be sinless. The question was once asked me in England by a friend, "Why should we look to the personality of a teacher?—we have only to judge of what he says, and takes that up." Not so. If a man wants to teach me something of dynamics or chemistry, or any other physical science, he may be anything he likes; he can still teach dynamics, or any other science. That is perfectly true, because the knowledge that the physical sciences require is simply intellectual, and depend on intellectual strength; a man can have in such a case a gigantic intellectual power without the least development of his soul. But in the spiritual sciences it is impossible from first to last that there can be any spiritual light in that soul which is impure. So what will he teach? He knows nothing. Spiritual truth is purity. "Blessed are the pure in heart, for they shall see God." In that one sentence is the gist of all religion. If you have learnt that, all that has been said in the past, and all that it is possible to say in the future, you have known; you need not look into anything else, for you have all that is necessary in that one sentence, it could save the world were all the other scriptures lost. A vision of God, a glimpse of the beyond, never come until the soul is pure. Therefore in the teacher of spirituality purity is the one thing that we must have, we must see *first* what he *is*, and *then* what he *says*. Not so with intellectual teachers of course, there we care more for what he says than what he is. With the teacher of religion we must first and foremost see what he is, and then alone comes the value of the words, because he is the transmitter. What will he transmit, if he has not that spiritual power in him? To give a simile—there is a certain vibration in the mind of the teacher which he conveys to the mind of the taught. If this heater here is hot, it can convey heat vibrations, but if not, it cannot. It is a question of transference, and not of stimulating only our intellectual faculties. Something real and tangible comes from the teacher, and goes to the taught, and begins to grow into a huge tree, therefore the first condition is that the teacher must be true.

Third is motive, look that he does not teach with any ulterior motive, for name, or fame, or any other motive, simply for love, pure love for you. When these spiritual forces are transmitted from the teacher to the taught, they can only be conveyed through the medium of love; there is no other medium that can convey them. Any other motive, such as gain or name, would immediately destroy the conveying medium; therefore all must be done through love. One who has known God; he alone can be a teacher. When you see that in the teacher these conditions are fulfilled, you are safe; if they are not fulfilled it is unsafe to be taught. There is a great danger if he cannot convey goodness, the danger of his conveying wickedness sometimes. This must be guarded against; therefore, it naturally follows that we cannot be taught anywhere and everywhere. Brooks preach sermons, and stones preach sermons is very true as a poetical figure, but no one can preach a single grain of truth until he has it in himself. To whom do the brooks preach sermons? To the human soul, the lotus of life that has been already opened, but the light comes from the teacher. When the heart has been opened it can receive teaching from the brooks, or the stars, or the moon, and so on; it can get some religious teaching from all these; but the unopened heart will see nothing but brooks and rolling stones. A blind man may go to a museum, but he only goes and comes; his eyes must be opened first, and then he learns. This eye-opener of religion is the teacher. With the teacher therefore, our relationship is that of the ancestor and descendant; the teacher is the spiritual ancestor, and the disciple is the spiritual descendant. It is all very well to talk of liberty and independence, and all these different things but not with the heart. Without that mildness, and submission, and veneration, and faith, there will not be any religion, and you will find it a significant fact that where this system still exists between the teacher and the taught, there alone gigantic spiritual souls grow, but in those who have thrown off this system, they make of religion just a lecture. The teacher expects his five dollars, and the taught expects to get his brain pan filled with the teacher's words, and when that is done I go my way and you go yours. In these nations and churches where this relation between teacher and taught is no longer maintained, spirituality is almost an unknown quantity ; it never comes without that feeling ; there is no one to transmit, in the first place, and no one to be transmitted to, in the second place, because they are all independent ; of whom can they learn, and if they come to learn, they come to *buy* learning. Give me a dollar's worth of religion ; cannot they pay dollars ? Religion cannot be got that way.

There is nothing higher and holier than this knowledge ; it comes to the soul. If a man has become a perfect Yogi it comes by itself, but it cannot be got in books. You may go and knock your head against the four corners of the world, the Himalayas, the Alps, the Çaucasus, the Desert of Gobi or Sahara, or the bottom of the sea, but it will not come, until you find a teacher. Find the teacher, serve him as a child, open your heart to his influence; see in him God manifested. Know him to be the teacher. That which fixes our attention on the teacher first is that for us he is the highest manifestation of God, and as the power of attention concentrates there that picture of the teacher melts and melts, the frame will vanish, and the real God will be left there.* Those that come to truth with such a spirit of veneration, of reverence, and love, for them the Lord of truth speaks the most wonderful words. "Take thy shoes from off thy feet, for the place whereon thou standest is holy ground." Wherever His name is spoken that place is holy. How much more so is a man who speaks His name, and with what veneration ought we to approach a man out of whom come spiritual truths. This is the spirit in which we are to be taught. Such teachers are few in number, no doubt, in this world, but the world is never without them. The moment it is absolutely bereft of these it will cease to be, it will become a hideous hell, and will just drop. These teachers are

*Hence the Salutation in India to-day to a Sannyasin *Namo Nârâyanâya!* Reverence to Deity (in thee)! and the Sannyasin's reply, *Nârâyana!* (Thou also art) Nârâyana (Deity), or Deity (is also in thee).

the fair flowers of human life, and keep the world going; it is the strength that is manifested from that heart of life that keeps the bonds of society intact. Beyond these is another set of teachers, the Christs of the world. They are the Teachers of all teachers, God Himself coming into the form of man. They are much higher; they can transmit spirituality with a touch, with a wish. The lowest, most degraded characters, in one second, become saints. Do you not read of how they used to do these things? They are not the teachers about whom I was speaking; they are the Teachers of all teachers; the greatest manifestation of God to man; we cannot see God, but through them. We cannot help worshipping them, and they are the only ones we are bound to worship.

No man hath "seen" God, only as He is manifested in the Son. We cannot see God. If we try to see Him we make a hideous caricature of God. There is a proverb in our language that an ignorant man was asked to make a metal image of the God Siva, and after days of struggle, he made an image of a monkey. So, whenever we attempt to make an image of God we make a caricature of Him, because we cannot understand Him as anything higher than man, as long as we are men. The time will come when we transcend our human nature, and know Him as He is, but as long as we are men we must worship Him in man. Talk as you may, try as you may, you cannot see God except as a man. You may deliver great intellectual speeches, become very great rationalists, and prove that these tales of God are all nonsense, but let us come to practical common sense. What is behind this remarkable intellect? Zero, nothing, simply so much froth. When next you hear a man delivering great intellectual lectures against this worship of God, get hold of him and ask him what is his idea of God, what he means by "omnipotence," and "omnipresence." and "omnipresent love," and so forth, beyond the spelling of the words. He means nothing, he cannot formulate an idea, he is no better off than a man in the street, who has not read a single book. That man in the street, however, is quiet and does not disturb the world, while the other man's arguments disturb the world. He has no actual perception, and both are on the same plane. Religion is realisation, and you must make the sharpest distinction between talk and realisation. What you perceive in your soul is realisation. Ask that man what is his idea of omnipotence, do you see omnipotence or Almighty God? What do you mean by this omnipresent Being? Man has no idea of the spirit, he has to think of it with the forms he has before him. He has to think of the blue skies, or the expansive fields, or the sea, or anything huge. How else can you think of God ? So what are you doing ? You are talking omnipresence, and thinking of the sea. Is God the sea ? Truce to all this frothy argument of the world, we want common sense. Nothing is so uncommon as common sense ; the world is too full of talk, therefore we are by our present constitution limited and bound to see God as man. If the buffaloes want to worship God, they will see Him as a huge buffalo. If a fish wants to worship God, it will have to form the idea of Him as a big fish, and if man, he will have to think of Him as man, and these are not imaginations. You and I, the buffalo, the fish, each represent so many different vessels. All these go to the sea to be filled up with water according to the shape of each vessel ; in the man according to the shape of a man, in the buffalo in the shape of a buffalo, in the fish in the shape of a fish. In each of these vessels is nothing but water. So with God. When men see Him, they see Him as man, and the animals as animal, with each according to his ideal. That is the only way you can see Him, you have to worship Him as this man, because there is no other way out of it. Two men do not worship

God as man—the human brute who has no religion, and the *Paramahamsa* (highest Yogî), who has gone beyond humanity has thrown off his mind and body, who has gone beyond the limits of nature. All nature has become his Self. He has neither mind nor body, and can worship God as God, as a Jesus or a Buddha. *They* did not worship God as man, The other extreme is the human brute. You will remember how two extremes meet; similarly with the extreme of ignorance and the other extreme of knowledge, neither of these worship anybody. The extreme of ignorance have realised themselves as God, they are God, whom will they worship? The other extreme has realised God, and God never worships God. Between these two poles of existence, if anyone tells you he is not going to worship God as man, take care of that man. He is an irresponsible talker, a mistake, his religion is for frothy thinkers, it is intellectual nonsense.

Therefore, it is absolutely necessary to worship God as man, and blessed are those r aceswhich have such a "God-man" to worship. Christians have such a God-man in Christ; therefore, cling close to Christ; never give up Christ. That is the natural way to see God; see God in man. All our ideas of God are concentrated there. The great limitation Christians have is, that they do not heed other manifestations of God—only Christ. He was a manifestation of God, so was Buddha, and there will be hundreds of others. Do not limit God anywhere. Pay all the reverence that you think is due to God, to Christ ; that is the only worship we can have. God cannot be worshipped ; He is the immanent Being of the universe, can He be ready to sit down with an apple in one hand, and a rod in the other. If you do good you get the apple, if you do wrong you get a stroke of the rod. It is only to His manifestation as man that we can pray. It is a very good plan if Christians pray to say "In the name of Christ." It would be a better idea to stop praying to God, and only to pray to Christ. God understands human failings and becomes a man to do good to humanity. "Whenever virtue subsides and immorality prevails, I come to help mankind," says Krishna. "Fools, not knowing that I, the omnipotent and omnipresent God of the universe, have taken this human form, deride me, and think how can that be." Their minds have been clouded with demoniacal ignorance, so they cannot see in Him the Lord of the universe. These great incarnations of God are to be worshipped. Not only so, they alone can be worshipped, and on the days of their birth, on the days when they went out of this world ; we ought to pay more particular reverence. In worshipping Christ I would rather worship Him just as He desires; on the day of His birth I would rather worship Him by fasting than by feasting—by praying. When these are thought of these great ones, they manifest themselves in our souls, and they make us like unto them. Our whole nature changes, and becomes like them. But you must not mix up Christ or Buddha with hobgoblins flying through the air, and all that sort of nonsense. Sacrilege! Christ coming into a spiritualistic *séance* to dance! I have seen that pretence in this country. It is not that way that these manifestations of God come, the very touch of one of them will be manifest upon a man; when Christ *touches*, the whole soul of man will change; that man will be transfigured just as He was. His whole life will be spiritualised; from every pore of his body spiritual power will emanate. What were the great powers of Christ in miracles, and healing, in one of His character? They were low, vulgar things that He could not help doing because he was among vulgar beings. Where was this miracle making done? Among the Jews; and the Jews did not take Him. Where was it not done? In Europe. The miracle-making went to the Jews, who rejected Christ, and the Sermon on the Mount to Europe, which accepted Him; the human spirit took on what was true, and rejected what was spurious. The great strength of Christ is not in His miracles or His healing; any fool could do that; fools can heal others; devils can heal others; I have seen horrible demoniacal men do wonderful miracles. They will manufacture fruits out of the earth. I have seen fools and diabolical men know the past, present and future. I have seen fools heal at a glance, by the will, the most horrible diseases. They are powers, truly, but often demoniacal powers. The other is the spiritual power of Christ, which will live, and always has lived, an almighty, gigantic love, and the words of truth which He preached. The action of healing men at a glance is forgotten, but His saying "Blessed are the pure in heart," that lives to-day. These words are a gigantic magazine of power, inexhaustible, so long as the human mind lasts. So long as the name of God is not forgotten these words will roll on, and on, and never cease. These are the powers Jesus taught, and the powers He had. The power of purity; it is a definite power. So in worshipping Christ, in praying to Him, we must always remember what we are seeking. Not those foolish things of miracle display, but the wonderful powers of the spirit, which maky man free, and give him control over the whole of nature, takes from him the badge of slavery, and shows God unto him.

CHAPTER IV.

Bhakti is divided into two portions. One is called *vaidhî*, the form or ceremonial; the other portion is called *mukhya*, supreme. The word *Bhakti* covers all the ground between the lowest form of worship and the highest form of life; all the worship that you have seen in any country in the world, or in any religion, is regulated by love. There is a good deal that is simply ceremony; there is a good deal which, though not ceremony, is still not love, a lower state still. Yet these ceremonies are necessary. This external part of *Bhakti* is absolutely necessary to help the soul onward. A great mistake is made by mankind, when they think that they can at once jump to the highest state; if a baby thinks he is going to be an old man in a day, he is mistaken, and I hope you will always bear in mind this one ideal, that religion is neither in books nor in intellectual consent, nor in reasoning. Reason, theories, documents, doctrines, books, religious ceremonies, are all *helps* to religion: religion itself consists of *realisation*. We all say, "There is a God." Have you seen God? That is the question. . ou hear everybody say, "There is a God in heaven." But ask them if they have seen Him, and if anyone says he has, you would laugh at him, and say he is a manaic. With most religion goes no further than a document, a sort of intellectual assent. I never preached such a religion in my life, and would not call it religion. It is better to be an atheist than to have that sort of religion. Religion does not depend on our intellectual assent, or dissent from something else. You say there is a soul. Have you seen the soul? How is it we all have souls and do not see them? You have to answer the question, and to find out the way to see the soul. If not, it is useless to talk of religion. If any religion is true it must be able to show us the soul, to show us God and the truth in ourselves. If you and I fight for all eternity upon one of these doctrines or documents we will never come to any conclusion. They have been fighting for ages, and what is the outcome? Intellect cannot reach there at all. We have to go beyond the intellect; the proof of religion is in direct perception. The proof of this wall is that we see it; if you sat down and argued about the existence or non-existence of that wall for ages, you would never come to any conclusion, but directly you see it, it is enough. If all the men in the world told you it did not exist you are not going to believe them, because you know that the evidence of your own eyes is superior to any amount of documents or doctrines in the world. All of you have probably read many books of Idealism, which say this world does not exist, and that you do not exist. You do not believe them, because they do not believe it themselves. They know that one witness of the senses overrules any amount of this stuff. To be religious you have first to throw books overboard, push them on one side. The less you read of books the better for you; do one thing at a time. It is a tendency in western countries, in these modern times, to make a hotch-potch of the brain; all sorts of unassimilated ideas running riot in the brain, and forming a chaos, without patience to form one real idea out of it. In many cases it becomes a sort of disease, but this is not religion at all. Then some want a nervous sensation. Tell them about ghosts, and people coming from the North Pole or any other remote place, with pairs of wings or in any other form, and that they are invisibly present and watching over them, and make their skins creep. Then they are satisfied and go home, but within twenty-four hours they are ready for a fresh sensation. This is what some call religion; this is the way to the lunatic asylum, and not to religion. If you go on in the same way for a century you will convert this country into a huge lunatic asylum. The Lord is not to be reached by the weak, and all these creepy things tend to weakness. Therefore touch them not with the toes of your feet; go not near them; they only make people weak, bring disorder to the brain, weaken the mind, demoralise the soul, and a hopeless muddle is the result. You must bear in mind that religion does not consist in talks, or doctrines, or books, but in realisation; it is not learning, but *being*. Everybody knows "Do not steal," but what of that? That man has really known, who has not stolen. Everybody knows "Do not injure others," but what value is that? Those who have not done so have realised it, they know it, and have built their character on it. So we have to realise religion, and this realisation of religion is a long process. Every man in this world has a tendency to think that he is the handsomest, and most powerful and learned, and most unique :being born. Every woman to think she is the most beautiful, and most intellectual thing born in the world. I yet hope to see a baby that is not extraordinary; every mother tells me that; her baby is so wonderful. This is human nature. When mankind hears of something very high and wonderful they all think they will get that, and never stop for a moment to consider that they will have to work their way up to it; they all jump there. If it is the highest, we are for it. We never stop to consider whether we have the power, and the result is that we do not do anything. You cannot take a man with a pitchfork and push him up there; we all have to work it out gradually; therefore the first part of religion is this *vaidhi* Bhakti, the lower phase of worship.

What are these lower phases of worship? They are various. To give you an example I will ask you one question. You all say there is a God, and that He is an omnipresent being. Close your eyes and think what He is. What do you find? Either you are thinking of the sea, or the blue sky, or an expanse of meadow, or such things as you have seen in your life. If that is so you do not mean anything by omnipresent God; it has no meaning at all. So with every other attribute of God. What idea have we of omnipotent, or omniscient? We have none. Religion is realising, and I will call you a worshipper of God, when you have become able to realise the idea. Before that it is the spelling of the word, and no more. So, in order to attain to this state where we can realise we must have to pass through the concrete, just as you see children often learn through the concrete first, and gradually come to the abstract. If you tell a baby five into ten is two, he will not understand it, but if you give him ten things he will understand it. It is a slow, long process. We are all of us babies here; we may be old, and have studied all the books in the universe, but we are all spirtual babies. It is this power of realisation that makes religion ; no amount of doctrines or philosophies, or ethical books, that you may have stuffed into your brain will matter much, only what you *are*, and what you have *realised*. In order to come to this realisation we must first find that we are babies. We have learnt the doctrines and documents, but nothing has been realised in our lives. We will have to begin now in the concrete, through forms and words, and prayers and ceremonies, and of these concrete forms there will be thousands ; one form need not be for everybody. Some are helped by images, some may not be. Some require a statue outside, others require an image inside the brain. The man who puts it inside says "I am a superior man ;" when it is inside it is all right ; when it is outside it is idolatry ; we will fight it. When a man puts an image in the form of a church or a temple he thinks it is holy, but when it is in the form of a human being he thinks it simply horrible. So there are various forms through which the mind will take this concrete exercise. and then, step by step, we will come to the abstract understanding, abstract realisation. Again the same form is not for everyone ; there is one form that will suit you, and another will suit somebody else, and so on. All forms, though leading to the same goal, may not be for all of us. Here is another mistake we generally make. My ideal does not suit you, why should I force it on you? My fashion of building churches or reading hymns does not suit you, why should I force it on you? Go into the world and every fool will tell you that his form is the only right one, that every other form is diabolical, and he is the only chosen man ever born in the universe. All these forms are good and helpful, and just as there are so many varieties in human nature, it is necessary there should be so many forms in religion, and the more there are the better for the world, If there are twenty forms of religion in the world it is very good, if there are 400 so much the better, there will be more to choose from. So we should rather be glad when the numbers of religions and religious ideas increase and multiply, because they are taking in every man, helping mankind more, and would to God they multiplied until every man had his own religion, quite separate from every other man. That is the idea of the Bhakti Yogi.

The final idea is that my religion cannot be yours, or yours mine, Although the goal and the aim are the same, yet each one has to take a different road, according to the idiosyncrasies of his mind, and although these roads are various they must all be true, because they lead to the same goal. It cannot be that one is true and the rest not. The choosing of one's own road in the language of Bhakti is called *ishtam*, the chosen way.

Then there are words. All of you have heard of this power of words ; how wonderful they are ; every book is full of the power of words—the Bible, the Qur'an, the Vedas. Certain words have wonderful power over humanity. Then there are other forms, symbols. Symbols have great influence on the human mind. But great symbols in religion were not created indefinitely. To illustrate that we will find that they are the natural expressions of the thought. We are always thinking symbolically. All our words are but symbols of the thought behind, and different people have come to use different symbols without knowing the reason why. It was all behind, and these symbols are associated with the thoughts, and as the thought brings the symbol outside, so the symbol, on the contrary. can bring the thought inside. So this portion of Bhakti tells about these various subjects of symbols and words and prayers. Every religion has prayers, but one thing you must bear in mind—praying for health, or wealth, are not *Bhakti*, they are all

Karma. Praying for any physical gain is simply *Karma,* such as a prayer for going to heaven and so forth. One that wants to love God, to be a Bhakta, must make a bundle of all these and throw them out of the door, and then enter. He who wants to enter the realms of light must make a bundle of all this buying and selling, "shop-keeping" religion, and then enter the gates. It is not that you do not get what you pray for ; you get everything, but it is low, vulgar, a beggar's religion. "Fool indeed is he who, living on the banks of the Ganges, digs a little well for water. Fool indeed is the man who, coming to a mine of diamonds, begins to search for glass beads." Beg God for health, dinner, or a piece of cloth. One is a mine of diamonds, and these are the glass beads of the world. This body will die some time, so what is the use of praying for its health again and again ? What is there in health and wealth ? The wealthiest man can use only a little portion of his wealth ; he cannot eat three dinners, he cannot wear more clothes, he cannot breathe more air than one man can. He cannot sleep upon more ground than it is possible for his length to cover. We can never get all the things of this world, and if not who cares ? This body will go, who cares for these things ? If good things come, welcome ; if they go away, welcome, let them go.

Blessed are they when they come, and blessed are they when they go. But to go and say, "Lord, take care of my glass, and, Lord, give me a jug, and, Lord, give me a new tie that is in fashion now," these are not *Bhakti*. They are the lowest states of religion. They are the lowest form of *Karma*. This is a higher thing; we are going to realise God. We are striving to come into the presence of the King of Kings. We cannot get there in a beggar's dress, in beggar's rags, with dirt and filth all about us. If we wanted to enter the presence of an emperor, would we be admitted? Certainly not. The lackeys would drive us out of the gates. This is the Emperor of Emperors, and in these beggar's rags we will not enter. Shop-keepers never have admission there; buying and selling will not do there at all. As you read in the Bible Jesus drove the buyers and sellers out of the Temple. "Lord I give you my little yrayer, and will give me a new dress. Lord, cure my head-ache; I'll pray two hours more to-morrow." Think yourselves a little higher than that! You are better than to be praying for little things like that; that is the difference between men and animals; all the potential mental energy of the animal is in his body. If a man uses all his mental energy in doing that, show me the difference between man and animal. So it goes without saying that the first task in becoming a Bhakta is to give up all these desires of heaven and so on. Such a heaven would be like these places here only a little better. We have here some miseries and some happiness, and all that. We will just have a little less, or a little more. There will be no more light than we have here; it will be the result of our good deeds; perhaps plenty to eat, or perhaps very little. Perhaps we will have the power to fly like bats through the air, and jump through walls, and play all sorts of tricks, or to dance in some *séance.* To my mind it is better to go to the nether regions than to run a spiritualistic camera. I would rather be compelled to find myself in the darkest end of earth than to be compelled to run spiritual *séances.* The Christian's idea of heaven is of a place of intensified enjoyment. How can that be God? You have perhaps been in such places hundreds of times, and tumbled down again. The question is how to get rid of these laws of nature. What makes men miserable? They are slaves, bound by these laws; puppets in the hand of nature, tumbled about like playthings. Look at a very big man, like an emperor. Presently hunger comes, and if he does not get a little food he begins to jump about and get mad. We are continually taking care of this body that anything can knock down, and so we are living in a constant state of fear. I was reading the other day the calculation of some man that a deer has to run on the average sixty or seventy miles every day because it gets frightened. It runs and runs for miles, and then stops and eats something. That man ought to have known that we are in a worse plight than the deer. The deer has some rest, and we have not. If the deer gets grass enough it is satisfied, but we are always multiplying our wants. It is a morbid desire with us to multiply our wants. We have become so unhinged and unnatural that nothing natural will satisfy us. Every nerve is full of poison and morbidity, and we are always grasping after morbid things, must have unnatural excitement and unnatural food and drink, and surroundings and life. The air must be poisoned first and then we can breathe. As to fear, what are our lives but bundles of fears? We are catching cold every day; we want food, one man says of one kind, and another of another. The deer has one set of things to fear, tigers, wolves, etc. Man has the whole universe.

How are we to break ourselves of this is the question. It is all very well to say we are men and human beings, I find utilitarians stand up and say, "Don't talk of God and all these things, we don't know anyting of these things, let us live happily in this world." I would be the first to do so if we could, but the world will not allow us. As long as you are a slave of nature how can you? The more you struggle the more enveloped you become. You are devising plans for I do not know how many years, and at the end of each one, things are worse. Two hundred years ago in the Old World people had few wants, but as their knowledge increased in arithmetical progression, so their wants increased in geometrical progression. We think that in salvation at least our desires will be fulfilled, so we want to get to heaven. This eternal, unquenchable thirst. Always wanting for something. When a man is a beggar he wants money, money, money. When he has money he wants other things, society, and after that something else. Never at rest. How are we to quench this? If we get to heaven it will only increase the desires. If a poor man gets rich it does not quench his desires, it is only like throwing butter on the fire, increasing its bright flames. Going to heaven is becoming intensely richer, and then the desires will come more and more. We read of many pranks played in heaven in the different Bibles of the world, they are not always very good there, and after all, this desire to go to heaven is a desire after enjoyment. This has to be given up. It is too little, too vulgar a thing to go to heaven, for you to think of. It is just the same as thinking I will become a millionaire and lord it over people. There are many of these heavens, and through them you will gain the right to enter the gates of religion and love.

CHAPTER V.

There are two Sanskrit words, one is called *Pratíka*, and the other is *Pratimá*. We will talk a little about this *Pratíka*, it means coming towards, nearing. In all countries you find various grades of worship. In this country, for instance, there are people who worship images of saints, there are people who worship certain forms and symbols. Then there are people who worship different beings higher than men, and their number is increasing very rapidly. Worshippers of departed spirits. I read that there are somewhere about eight millions of them here. Then there are other people who worship certain higher grade beings, the angels, the gods, and so forth. Bhakti Yoga does not condemn any one of these various grades, but they are all classed under one name, *Pratíka*, worship of the *Pratíka*. They are not worshipping God, but *Pratíka*, something which is near, struggling towards God through all these things. This *Pratíka* worship cannot lead us on to salvation and freedom, it can only give us certain particular things for which we worship them. For instance, if a man worships his departed ancestors, or departed friends, perhaps he may get certain powers or certain information from them; any particular gift that is got from these objects of worship is called *vidyâ*, particular knowledge, but freedom, the highest aim, comes only by worship of God Himself. Some Orientalists think, in expounding the Vedas, that even the personal God, Himself, is a *Pratîka*, but it does not mean that. A personal God is the same as a *Pratika*, but the *Pratikas* are neither personal nor impersonal God. They cannot be worshipped as God. So, it would be a great mistake if people thought that by worshipping these different *Pratikas*, either as angels, or ancestors, or holy men (Mahatmas, saints, etc.), or departed sprits, they could ever reach to freedom. At best they can only reach to certain powers, but God alone can make us free. But because of that they are not to be condemned, they each one will have a result, and the man who does not understand anything higher will get some power, some enjoyment, from these *Pratikas*, and, after a long course of experience, when he will be ready to come to freedom, he will naturally give up all these *Pratikas*.

Of all these various *Pratikas* the most prevalent form is that of worshipping departed friends. Human nature, personal love, love for the bodies of our friends, is so strong in us, that, when they die, we are always trying to see their bodies once more,—clinging on to the bodies. We forget that these bodies while living were constantly changing, and when they die, we think they are become constant, and that we shall see them so. Not only so, but if I have a friend, if I have a child, who has been a blackguard, as soon as he dies I begin to think he is the saintliest person in existence, he becomes a God. There are people in India who, if a baby dies, do not burn him, but put him under the ground, bury him, and build a temple over him, and that little baby becomes the God of that temple. This is a very prevalent form of religion in any country, and there are not wanting philosophers who think this has been the origin of all religions. Of course they cannot prove it. We must remember, however, that this worship of *Ptatikas*, can never bring us to salvation or to freedom. Secondly it is very dangerous. The danger is that these *Pratikas*, "nearing-stages," so far as they lead us on to a further stage, are all right, but it is ninety-nine to one that we will stick to the *Pratikas* all our lives. It is a very good to be born in a church, but it is a very bad to die in a church. To make it clearer, it is very good to be born in a certain training, a certain sect; it bring us out, but in the vast majority of cases we die in that little sect, we never come out, or grow. That is the great danger of all these worships of *Pratikas*.

Men will tell you that they are all stages through which they are passing, but when they are old they still stick to them. If a young man does not go to a church he ought to be condemned, but if an old man goes to a church he, also, ought to be condemned, he has no business with this child's play any more, the church should have been merely a preparation for something higher. What business has he any more with forms and *Pratikas*, and all these preliminaries.

Book worship is another strong form of this *Pratika*, the strongest form. You find in every country that the book becomes the God. There are sects in my country who believe that God incarnates and becomes man, but even God as incarnate man must conform to the Vedas, and if His teachings do not so conform they will not take them. Buddha is worshipped by all the sects, but if you say to them "If you worship Buddha, why don't you take his teachings?" they will say because it denies the Vedas. Such is the meaning of book worship. Any number of lies under cover of a book are all right. In India if I want to teach anything new, and simply state it on my own authority, as what I think, nobody will come to listen to me, but if I take some passage from the Vedas, and juggle with it, and give it the most impossible meaning, murder everything that is reasonable in it, and bring out my own ideas as the ideas that were meant by the Vedas, all fools will follow me in a crowd. Then there are men preaching a roaring sort of Christianity that would frighten the ordinary Christian out of his wits, but they say "this is what Jesus Christ meant," and all the fools come round them. People do not want anything new, if it is not in the Vedas or the Bible. It is a case of nerves; when you hear a new and striking thing you are startled or when you see a new thing you are startled, it is constitutional. It is much more so with thoughts. The mind has been running in ruts, and to take up a new idea is too horrible, so the idea has to be put near the ruts, and then we slowly take it. It is good policy, but bad morality. Think of the mass of lies that these reformers tell, and what you call the liberal preachers are pouring into society today, fully conscious that they are telling lies; they know full well there was no such meaning, but if they did not preach them none would come near them. According to Christian Scientists Jesus was a great healer, according to the Spiritualists He was a great ghost producer, according to the Theosophists he was a Mahatma. All these have to be deduced from the same text. There is a text in the Vedas which says "Existence *(Sat)* alone existed, oh, beloved, nothing else existed in the beginning." Many different meanings are given to the word *Sat* in this text. The Atomists say the word meant "atoms," and out of these atoms the world has been produced. The Naturalists say it meant "nature," and out of nature everything has come. The Sunya-Vadins (maintainers of the Void) say it meant "nothing," "zero" and out of nothing everything has been produced. The Theists say it means "God," and the Advaitists say it was Absolute Existence, and all refer to the same text as their authority. These are the defects of book worship, but there is a great advantage in it, it gives strength. All the various religious sects have disappeared excepting those that have a book. Nothing seems to kill them. Some of you have heard of the Parsees. They were the ancient Persians, and at one time there were about a hundred millions of them. They were conquered by the Arabs, and modern Parsees have become Mohammedans. They had a book and that travelled all over the world and that having a book preserved them. A book is the most tangible form of God. Think of the Jews; if they had not had a book they would have simply melted into the world, but that keeps them on; the Talmud keeps them in spite of the most horrible persecution. That is one of the great advantages of a book, that it crystallises everything in a very nice tangible form, and it is the handiest of all idols. Just put a book on an altar and everyone sees it; a good book everyone reads. I am afraid I may be a little partial, but in my opinion books have produced more evil than good. They are accountable for all these doctrines. Creeds all come from books, and books are alone responsible for the persecution and fanaticism in the world. Books in modern times are making liars eveywhere. I am astonished at the number of liars abroad in every country.

The next thing to be considered is the *Pratimâ*, image, the use of images. All over the world you will find images in some form or other. With some it is in the form of a man, and that is the best form. If I wanted to worship an image I would worship it in the form of a man, rather than of an animal, or a building, or any other form. One sect thinks this is the right sort of image, and another thinks it is bad. The Christian thinks that when God came in the form of a dove it was all right, but if He comes in the form of a cow, as the Hindus say, it is very wrong and superstitious. The Jews think if an idol be made in the form of a chest with two angels sitting on it, and a book in it, it is all right, but if it is in the form of a man or a woman it is very horrible.

The Mahommedans think that when they pray, if they try to form an image of the temple with the Kaba, the black stone, in it, and turn towards the west, it is all right, but if you form the image in the shape of a church it is idolatry. This is the defect of image worship. Yet all these seem to be necessary stages, except book worship. That is very wicked; we had better be rid of that, and instead of them to think what we ourselves believe. What you have realised is the question. What Jesus, or Buddha, or Moses did is nothing to us, unless we too do it for ourselves. It would not satisfy your hunger to shut yourselves up in a room and think of what Moses ate, neither will what Moses thought save *you*. My ideas are very radical on these points. Sometimes I think that I am right when I am agreeing with all these ancient teachers, at other times I think they are right when they agree with me. So I ask you all to think that way, Be entirely free from these holy teachers; pay all reverence to them, but look at religion as an independent research. I have to find my light, just as they found theirs. Their finding the light will not satisfy us at all. You have to *become* the Bible, and not to follow it, excepting as paying reverence to it, as a light on the way, guide posts, marks. That is all the value they have, but these images and other things are quite necessary. You may try to bring your mind to concentrate, or even to project any thought. You will find that you will naturally form images in your mind. You cannot help it. Two sorts of persons never require any images—the human animal who never thinks of any religion, and the perfected being who has passed through these stages. Between these two points all of us require some sort of ideal outside and inside. It may be in the form of a departed human being, or of a living man or woman. This is clinging to personality, and bodies, and is quite natural. We are prone to concretise. Why should we be here if we are not concretised? We are concreted spirits, and so we find ourselves here on this earth. Idols have brought us here, and they will take us out. It is the homœopathic cure, *simila similibus*. Going after things of the senses has made us human beings, and we are bound to worship personal beings, whatever we may talk. It is very easy to say "Don't be personal," but the same man you will find most personal. His attachment for particular men and women is very strong; it will not leave him when they die, but he wants to follow them beyond death. That is idolatry; it is the seed, the very cause of idolatry, and the cause being there it will come out in some from. Is it not better to have a personal attachment to an image of Christ or Buddha than to a living wicked man or woman? The Americans say it is very bad to kneel before an image of Christ, but they say it is the highest thing to kneel before a woman, and say "You are my life, the light of my life, the light of my eyes, my soul." If they had four legs they would kneel on all four. That is worse idolatry than anything. Animals will kneel that way. What is this talk about my soul, my life? In five days it will go away. It is only attachment of the sexes. Why does not man kneel to men if it is not so? It is lust covered by a mass of flowers, the same as you find in brutes. Poets give it a good name, and through levender water and all sorts of things over it, but it is lust. Is it not better to kneel before a statue of Buddha, the Jina conqueror, and say "*Thou* art my life." I would rather a hundred times do that than kneel to any woman.

There is another sort of *Pratika* which is not in western countries, but which is in our books. They will teach the worship of mind as God. Worship this and that as God, they are each a stage, a nearing. An example is that of the man who wanted to see the pole star. He was shown a big star near to it, called "Arundhati," and when he had fixed his attention on that, and had got to know it he was shown the next finest star, and when he had fixed his attention on that he got to the pole star. So all these various *Pratikas* and *Pratimâs* lead to that. The worship of Bhddha and Christ are all *Pratika*, coming near to the worship of God, but the worship of Buddha and of Christ would not save a man, he must go beyond that. He who manifested God. is Jesus Christ, but God alone can give us freedom. There are some philosophers who say these should be made God; they are not *Pratikas*, but God Himself. We can take all these different *Pratikas*, these stages, and not be hurt by them; but if we think while we are worshipping these *Pratikas* we are worshipping God, we are mistaken. If a man worships Jesus Christ, and thinks he will be saved by that, he is mistaken entirely. If a man thinks that by worshipping departed ghosts or spirits he will be saved, he is entirely mistaken, or by worshipping an idol. But you can worship anything by seeing God *in* it, if we can forget the idol and see God there. You must not project anything upon God, but inject God into anything you like. You can worship God in a cat. Forget the cat and you are all right, because "out of Him comes everything." He is everything. We can worship a picture as God, but not God as that picture. God *in* the picture is all right, but the picture as God is wrong. God in a cat is perfectly right; there is no danger in that. But the cat God is a *Pratika*. The first is just the real worship of God.

The next great thing to consider in *Bhakti* is the "word." We talked on the teacher the other day. There is another great form of Bhakti Yoga, the *namasakti*, the power of the name. The whole universe is composed of name and form. Either it is a compound of name and form, or it is simply name, and the form is the mental image. So, after all, there is nothing that is not name and form. We all see God as without form or shape, but as soon as we begin to *think* of Him, He gets both name and form. The *chitta* is like the calm lake, and thoughts are like the waves upon the *chitta*, and name and form are the normal ways in which these waves will rise; no wave can rise without name and form. The uniform cannot be thought; it must be beyond thought, but as soon as it becomes thought and matter, it must have name and from. We cannot separate them. It is said in many books that God created this universe out of word. *Shabdhabrahma* in Sanskrit is the Christian theory of word. It was an old Indian theory, was taken to Alexandria by Indian preachers and got planted there. Thus the idea of word and incarnation became fixed there. There is deep meaning in the thought that God created everything out of word. God Himself being formless when these forms were projected, this is the best thing to say about the Creation. The Sanskrit word for Creation is *sristi*, projection. What nonsense is meant by "God created things out of nothing"? The universe is projected out of God. He becomes the universe, and it all returns to Him, and again it proceeds forth and again returns. For eternity it will go on that way. We have seen that this projection of anything in your mind cannot be without name and form. Suppose your mind is perfectly calm, entirely thoughtless, as soon as thought begins it will immediately take name and form. It has a certain name and a certain form. So the very fact of creation, the very fact of projection is eternally connected with name and form. Thus we find that every idea that man has, or can have, must be connected with a certain word as its counterpart. This being so, it is quite natural to suppose that this universe is the outcome of mind, just as your body is the outcome of your idea, as it were, made concrete and externalised. If it be true, moreover, that the whole universe is built on the same plan, then if you know the manner in which one atom is built, you can understand how the whole universe is built. If it is true, that in your own body, the body forms the concrete form, and the idea forms the finer part inside, and both are eternally inseparable, then, when you cease to have the body, you will cease to have the mind also. You can see that every day. When a man's brain is getting disturbed his ideas also get disturbed, because they are but one, the finer and the grosser parts. There are not two such things as matter and mind. Take a column of air forty miles high, and if we go up and up it becomes more rarefied as we go up, it becomes more and more subtle. So it is with this body. It is one thing throughout, only layer on layer, from grosser to finer. It is as the nails. We cut them off and again they grow. The body is the same. The finer the form the more persistent it is; we will find that always. The grosser it is the less persistent. So we find the form is the grosser and the name the finer. But these three are one; it is the Unity and the Trinity, the three degress of existence of the same thing. Finer, more condensed, and most condensed. Whenever the one is the others are there also. Wherever name is, there is form and idea. It naturally follows that if this universe is built upon the same plan as this body, this universe must have these three things—form, name, and thought. That thought is the finest part of the universe, the real motive power, and that is called God. That thought behind our body is called soul, and the thought behind the universe is called God. Then after that is the name, and last of all is the form which we see and feel. Just as you are a particular person, a little universe in this universe, there is a body which has a particular form, then behind that is the name, Mr. S. or Mrs. S. and behind that is the idea. Similarly there is this whole universe, that you multiply until it became infinite, and behind that is the name, and that is the name which projected this external; that name is what is called the "word" in all religions. "In the beginning was the word, and the word was with God, and the word was God." That name takes form, and behind that is God. The universal thought, *mahat*, as the Sankhyas call it, universal consciousness. What is that name? There must be some name. We see it. It is reasonable, most perfect logic. I do not see any flaw in it. The world is perfect and complete, and modern science shows beyond doubt that each atom is composed of the same material as the whole universe. If you know one lump of clay you know the whole universe, to know the whole universe you have simply to take a little bit of clay and analyse it. If you know this table *perfectly*, in all its bearings, you know the whole universe. Man is the most representive being in the universe, the microcosm, a small universe in himself. So in man we find there is the form, behind that the name, and behind that the thought, the thinking being. So this universe must be on exactly the same plan. The question is what is that name? According to the Hindus that word is *Om*. The Egyptains also belived that, the old Egyptians. "Seeking *Om* they give up the universe, I will tell you in short what He is, He is *Om*." "This is Brahman himself, this is the ancient One, and He who knows the secret of this *Om*, whatever he desires he gets."

So far about the universe. Now we come to different nanifestations. This *Om* stands for the name of the whole universe, or God. It stands midway between the external world and God, represents both. But then we can take the universe piecemeal, according to the different senses, as touch, as colour, as taste, and in various ways. In each case it is necessary that we make of this universe millions of universes from different standpoints, and each standpoint will be a complete universe by itself, and each one will have a name and a form and the thought behind. These thoughts behind are these *Pratikas*. They are the concrete *Pratikas*, the concrete layers of the particular universe, and there will be name behind each *Pratîka.* There are various names of sacred words, and these are used in Bhakti Yoga. So far as to the theory of the name, and what of the use? These names have almost infinite power. Simply by repetition of these words we can get anything we desire, we can come to perfection. But two things are necessary. "The teacher must be wonderful, so also must be the taught." These names must come from a person to whom it has come through right succession. From master to disciple, the spiritual current, as it were, coming from most ancient time, and these are bearing their power with them when they come from teachers to the disciples, and when repeated they become almost infinite power. The person from whom such a word comes is called a Guru, and the person to whom it goes is called Sishya, the disciple. When the word has been received in the regular way, and when it has been repeated, everything has been done in Bhakti Yoga. Simply by the repetition of that word will come the highest state of Bhakti. "You have so many names. You understand what is meant by them, and all these names are Thine, and in each name is Thy infinite power, there is neither time nor place for repeating these names, for every time is holy and every place is holy.

Thou art so easy, Thou art so merciful, how unfortunate am I, that I have no love for Thee."

CHAPTER VI.

The theory of *Ishtam*, about which we spoke in our last, is something to which I hope you will give careful attention, because with a proper understanding of this, we can understand all the various religions of the world. The word *Ishtam* is derived from the root of the root Isha, to desire, choose. The ideal of all religions, all sects, of mankind is the same, attaining to liberty, and cessation of misery. Wherever you find religion, you find these two ideals working in one or other form. Of course in lower stages of religion and of mankind they are not so well expressed, but still, well or ill-expressed, they are the one goal to which everyone of us is approaching, we want to get rid of misery, our daily misery, and so forth, and we are struggling to attain to liberty, physical, mental, spiritual. This is the whole idea upon which the world is working. The goal being the same there may be many ways to reach it, and these ways are determined by the peculiarities of our nature. One man's nature is emotional, another's is intellectual, another's is active, and and so forth. Again in the same nature, there will be so many sub-divisions, love, for instance, with which we are specially concerned in this

Bhakti class. One man's nature has a stronger love for children, another for wife, another for mother, another for father, another for friends. Another has love for country, and a few love humanity in the broadest sense, they are of course very few ; I do not think there are more than a hundred all over the world at the present moment, although everyone of us talks of it as if it were the guiding motive power of our lives. Some few sages have experienced it, and out of that experience have coined the word, and gradually it has become common, and fools take it up, and just as their brains are vacant they talk these words without any meaning. So we have a few great souls among mankind who feel this universal love, and out of their feeling people like me take up the feeling and preach about it. That is the fate of all great things, but let us hope that in the course of time more will come, and that this world will never be without such men, though few perhaps they be. To return to the subject. We find that even in one subject there will be so many various ways of attaining to its goal. All Christians believe in Christ, but think how many different explanations they have of Him. Each branch sees Him in different lights, from different standpoints of view. If you ask a Presbyterian what was Christ, his eyes are fixed upon that scene in Christ's life when He went to the money changers; they look on Him as a fighter. If you ask a Quaker, perhaps he will say "He forgave His enemies." The Quaker takes that view, and so on. If you ask a Roman Catholic what point of Christ's life is the most pleasing to him, he, perhaps, will say "When He gave the keys to Peter." Each one sect is bound to see Him in its own way. It follows that there will be so many divisions and sub-divisions even in the same subject. Ignorant persons take one of these sub-divisions and take their stand upon it, and they not only deny the right of every other man to interpret the universe according to his own light, but dare to say that others are entirely wrong, and they alone are right. If they are opposed they begin to fight. They say that they will kill any man who does not believe as they believe. Just as the Mahommedans do, and as Christians are even now doing in different countries. These are people who think they are sincere, and who ignore all others. But what is the position we want to take in this Bhakti Yoga? Not only that we would not tell others they are wrong, but tell them they are right, all of these who follow their own ways. That way which your nature makes it absolutely necessary for you to take, is the right way. Each one of us is born with a peculiarity of nature as the result of our past existence. Either you call it your own reincarnated past experience, or a hereditary past. Whatever way you may put it, we are the result of the past, that is absolutely certain, if anything is, through whatever channels that past has come. It naturally follows that each one of us is one effect, of which our past has been the cause, and as such there is a peculiar movement, a peculiar train, in each one of us, and therefore each one will have to find a way for himself. This way, this method, to which each of us is naturally adapted is called the "chosen way." This is the theory of *Ishtam*, and that way which is ours we call our own *Ishtam*. For instance, one man's idea of God is the omnipotent ruler of the universe. His nature is perhaps such. He is an overbearing man who wants to rule everyone, he naturally finds God an omnipotent ruler. Another man, who was perhaps a schoolmaster, and severe, cannot see any but a just God, a God of punishment and so on. Each one sees God according to his own nature, and this vision, conditioned by our own nature, is oru *Ishtam*. We have brought ourselves to a position where we can see that vision of God, and that alone, we cannot see any other vision. You will perhaps sometimes think of the man who taught you, and think that his teaching is the best, and fits you exactly, and the next day you ask one of your friends to go and hear him, and he comes away with the idea it was the worst teaching he had ever heard. He is not wrong, and it is useless to quarrel with him. The teaching was all right, but it was not fitted to that man. To extend it a little further we must understand that truth can be truth, and at the same time false. This would appear at first like a contradiction, but we must rememer that an absolute truth is only one, but in all relative truths it must be various. Take your vision of this universe for instance. This universe is an absolute entity, is unchangeable and unchanged, and the same throughout. But you and I and each of us hear, and see each one his own universe. Take the sun. The sun is an absolute entity, is one unchangeable universe, but you and I and a hundred other people may stand and look at it, and each one of us see a different sun. We are bound to see a different vision of the sun. A little change of place will make a change of vision of the sun for the same man. A little change in the atmosphere will make a different vision. So for relative perceptions, truth always appears various. But the absolute truth is only one. Therefore you need not fight with others when you find they are telling something about religion which is not exactly as your view of it. You ought to remember that both of you may be true, thoug apparently contradictory. There may be millions of radii approaching towards the same centre of the sun, and the further they are from the centre the distance between any two radii is greater, and as all these converge to the centre all difference vanishes. This centre is the absolute goal of mankind. The centre is there, but one and all of these radii branching out, are the constitutional limitations through which alone we can have a vision of it, and while standing on this plane we are bound each one of us to have a different view of this absolute reality, and as such we are all true, and no one need quarrel with the other. The only solution will be to approach the centre. If we find that hundreds of us differ in our opinion and we sit down and try to settle those differences by argument or quarrelling, we shall find that we can go on for hundreds of years without coming to a conclusion. History proves that. The only solution is to march ahead and go towards the centre, and the sooner we do that the sooner our differences vanish.

This theory of *Ishtam*, therefore, is allowing a man to choose his own religion. You cannot worship what I worship, nor I what you worship; it is impossible, and all these attempts to herd together human beings, and by means of armies or of arguments or force to drive them pell-mell into the same enclosure, and make them worship the same God, have failed, and will fail always, because it is constitutionally impossible. Not only so. There is the danger of destroying people. You scarcely meet any man or woman who is not struggling for some sort of religion, and how many are satisfied, or rather how few are satisfied, how few find anything, and why? Simply because all these are going for impossible tasks. They are forced into these methods by the diction of others. For instance, I am born a child, and my father puts a little book into my hand and says God is such, and such, and this is such and such. What business has he to put that into my mind? How does he know what way I will develop? And being ignorant of my constitutional development he wants to force his ideas on my brain, and the result is I shall not grow. You cannot make a plant grow on nothing or on soil unsuited to it. The day you can grow a plant out of nothing, you will be able to teach a child. A child teaches itself. But you can *help* it to go along in its own way. What you can do, is not of the positive nature, but the negative. You can take away the obstacles, but knowledge comes out of its own nature. Loosen the soil a little, so that it can come out easily. Put a hedge round it; see that it is not killed by anything else, by frost and snow, and there your work stops. You cannot do anything else. The rest is a manifestation *within* its own nature. So with the education of a child; a child educates himself. You are coming to hear me, and when you go home, compare what you have learned, and you will find you have thought out the same thing; I have only given it expression. I can never teach you anything: you will have to teach yourself, but I can help you perhaps in giving expression to that thought. So in religion—more so—I must teach myself religion. What right had my father to put all sorts of nonsense into my head? What right has my master to put these things into my head? What right has society to put these things into my head? Perhaps they are good, but they may not be *my* way. Think of the appalling evil that is in the world to-day, of the millions and millions of innocent children killed out. How many beautiful things which would have become wonderful spiritual truths have been nipped in the bud by this horrible idea of family religion, and social religion, and country religion, and so forth. Think of what a mass of superstitions is in your head just now about your childhood's religion, or your country's religion. Not only have they half killed you and destroyed you, but you are ready this moment to kill your own children. Man does not know what an amount of evil he does, and can do, and it is well he cannot, for if he knew it once, he would commit suicide. He does not know what a potent power lies behind each thought and action. The old saying is true that "fools rush in where angels fear to tread." This is to be avoided from the very first. How ? By this belief in *Ishtam.* There are so many ideals ; I have no right to say what shall be your ideal, to force any ideal on you. My duty should be to lay before you all these ideals, and enable you to see by your own constitution what you like best, and which is most fitted to you. Take up any one and persevere with that ideal, and what you have taken up is called your *Ishtam*, your special ideal. We see then that a congregational religion can never be. The *real* work of religion must be everyone's individual private business. I have an idea of my own ; I must keep it sacred and secret, because I know that it need not be your idea. Secondly why should I create a disturbance by telling everyone what is my idea ? Other people would come and fight me. The world is full of fools and lunatics. Sometimes I think it is a great lunatic asylum, this world of ours ! It is God's menagerie ! They cannot quarrel with me if I do not tell them, but if I go about telling them what my ideas are they will all be opposing me. So what is the use of telling then? This *Ishtam* should be kept secret to everyone of you. What is your own business is not others' business to know; that is between you and God. All theoretical portions of religion can be preached in public, and made congregational, but when higher religion comes in, it cannot be done in public. I cannot get ready my religious feelings at five minutes' notice. What is the result of this mummery and mockery? It is making a joke of religion, the worst of blasphemy. The result is that churches are places where ladies go to show their dresses, and instead of being places where they get married, they are becoming places where they show themselves on before they get married. How can human beings stand this religious drilling? It is like soldiers in a barrack. Shoulder arms, kneel down, take a book, all regulated exactly. Two minutes of feeling, two minutes of reason, two minutes of prayer, all arranged beforehand. These are horrible things, and should be avoided from the very first. These mummeries have driven out religion, and if continued for a few centuries, religion will cease to be. What shall remain to the churches? Let them preach doctrines, theories, philosophy to their hearts' content, but when it comes to worship, the real practical part of religion, it is just as Jesus says, "Go into your room and close the door, and pray in secret."

This is the theory of *Ishtam*. As you think of it, you will find it is the only way to make religion practically meet the necessities of different states of constitution, to avoid quarrelling with others, and to make real practical progress in spiritual life. But I must warn you that you do not misconstrue my words into the formation of secret societies. If there were a devil I would look at the door of a secret society for him, as the invention of secret societies. They are diabolical schemes. This is *sacred*, not secret. Why should you not speak of your *Ishtam* to other? Because it is your sacred thing. It may help others, but how do I know that it will not hurt others? There may be a man whose nature is such that he cannot worship a Personal God, but can only worship as an impersonal God, his own highest Self. Suppose I leave him among you and he tells you that there is no Personal God, but only God as you or I. You will be shockcd. His idea is sacred, but not secret. There never was a great religion, or a great teacher, who formed secret societies to preach God's truths. There are no such secret societies in India, they are all your Western ideas, and which they want to foist upon India. We never knew anything about them, and why should there be secret societies in India? In Europe a man was not allowed to talk a word about religion that did not agree with the views of the Church. So these poor fellows were forced to go about in mountains, hiding, and forming secret societies, so that they might follow their own kind of worship. There was never a time when any man in India was persecuted for holding different views on religion from others. There were never secret religious societies in India until the Europeans went there, so any idea of that sort you must give up at once. It is the most horrible thing that you can imagine, and it always degenerates into the most horrible things. I know enough of this world to know what they mean, and how easily they slide into free love societies and ghost societies, and then they come to seeking out each others' affinities, how men swear away their lives, their future possibilities of growth in thought and act into the hands of other men or women, and so on. Some of you may be displeased with me for talking in this way, but I have to tell you the truth. Half a dozen men and women will hear me all my life, perhaps; but they must be real men and women, pure and sincere, and I do not want a crowd. What can crowds do? The history of the world was made by a few dozen, whom you can count on your fingers, and the rest were a rabble, All these secret societies and humbugs make men and women impure, weak, and narrow ; and the weak have no will, and can never work, Therefore have nothing to do with them. All these are suppressed lust or false love of mystery, and should be knocked on the head the first time they come into your mind. No one who is the least impure will ever become religious. Do not try to cover festering sores with masses of roses. Do you think you can cheat God? None can. Give me every day a straightforward man or woman, but Lord save me from all these ghosts, flying angels and devils coming from the bowels of the earth. Be every-day, common, nice people. You must always remember this when you come in contact with these superhuman claims.

There is such a thing as instinct in us in common with the animals, mechanical movement of the body. There is a higher form of guidance, which we call reason, when intellect gets facts and then generalises them. There is a still higher form of knowledge which we call inspiration, which does not reason, but knows things by a flash. That is the highest form. But how do you know it from instinct? That is the great difficulty. Every fool comes to you, nowadays, and says he is inspired. "I have an inspiration, so build me a pedestal, crowd round me, and worship me." How are you to know whether it is an inspiration or a blackguardism? In the first place the first test of inspiration is that it must not contradict reason. The old man does not contradict the child, he is the developent of the child; what we call inspiration is the development of reason. The way to intuition is through reason. Inspiration must not contradict reason; where it does, throw it overboard. Instinctive movements of your body do not cross reason. As you cross a street how instinctively you move your body to save yourself from the cars. Does your mind tell you it was foolish to save your body that way? It does not. No genuine inspiration will ever contradict reason. Where it does it is all humbug. Secondly, this inspiration must be for the good of one and all; it shall be for the good of men and not for name and fame, or for filling the pocket of some blackguard. It shall always be for the Good of the world, perfectly unselfish, good to humanity, and when these tests are fulfilled you are quite safe to take it as inspiration. Thirdly you must remember that there is not one in millions that is inspired in the present state of the world. I hope there will be many more, and that each one of you will be so. We are now only playing with religion, and then alone will we begin to have religion. Just as Paul says. "For now we see through a glass darkly, but then face to face." But in the present state of the world they are few and far between that attain to that state, and at no other period were such humbug claims made to inspiration as now, and in no country more than in the United States. They all claim that women have intuitive faculties, and men are slowly dragging through reason. Do not believe in these tall talks. There are just as many inspired men as women ; women have more claim to peculiar forms of hysterics and nervousness. You had better die a tremendous unbeliever. than be played upon by cheats and jugglers. This little reason was given you, so show that you have used it properly. Then you will be able to take care of higher things.

[The Swami mentioned an instance of a Southern Hindu. well educated, but misled by stories of remarkable men dwelling in the Himalayas, (Mahatmas) and who was offended, and regarded him as an impostor when told that he knew nothing of any such beings, and that there was in all probability no truth in such tales.]

Such is the world, and when these fools tell

you one story the only way is to tell them another bigger one. It is a disease, a morbid desire. It degenerates the race, weakens the nerves and the brain, living in incessant morbid fear of hobgoblins, or stimulating the hunger for wonders; all these wild stories keep the nerves at unnatural tension. Slow and sure degeneration of the race.

We must always remember that God is Love, and none of these things. "Fool indeed is he who living on the banks of the Ganges wants to dig a little well for water. Fool indeed is the man who living near a mine of diamonds spends his life in searching for beads of glass." God is that mine of diamonds. We are fools indeed to give up God for legends of ghosts of flying hobgoblins, or flying machines, and all sorts of nonsense. It is degradation, the very thing is filthy to talk about, and to think of giving up God, and purity, and holiness, and spirituality, to go after all this nonsense! Reading other men's thoughts! If I have to read everybody's thoughts for five minutes I will go crazy. Be strong and stand up and seek the God of Love. This is the highest strength. What power is higher than the power of purity? Love and purity govern the world. This love of God cannot be reached by the weak. therefore be not weak, either physically, or mentally, or morally, or spiritully. All these things simply make you weak; therefore they must be shunned. The Lord alone is true; everything else is untrue; everything else should be rejected. Vanity of Vanities, all is vanity. Serve the Lord and Him alone.

CHAPTER VII.

PREPARATORY AND SUPREME BHAKTI YOGA.*

The idea of a Personal God has obtained in almost every religion, except a very few. With exception of the Buddhist and the Jain, perhaps, all the religions of the world have had the idea of a Personal God, and with it, comes the idea of devotion and worship. These two religions, the Buddhist and the Jain, although they have no Personal God to worship, have taken up the founders of their religions, and worship them precisely in the same way as others worship a Personal God. This idea of devotion and worship of some being who has to be loved, and who can reflect back the love to man is universal. This idea of love and devotion is manifested in various degrees, and through different stages, in various religions. The lowest stage is that of ritualism, when man wants things that are concrete, when abstract ideas are almost impossible, when they are dragged down to the lowest plane, and made concrete. Forms come into play, and along with them various symbols. Throughout the history of the world we find that man is trying to grasp the abstract through thought forms or symbols,

*This address was delivered at Madison Square Concert Hall, New York, February 9th, 1896.

and all the external manifestations of religions—bells, music, rituals, books and images—all come under that head. Anything that appeals to the senses, anything that helps man to form a concrete image of the abstract, is taken hold of and worshipped.

There have been reformers in every religion, from time to time, who have stood against all symbols and rituals, but vain have been their attempts, for we find that so long as man will remain as he is, the vast majority of mankind will always want something concrete to hold on to, something around which, as it were, to place their ideas, something which will be the centre of all the thought forms in their minds. The great attempts of the Mahommedans, and of the Protestants (among the Christians) have been directed to this one end, of doing away with all rituals, and yet we find that even with them rituals creep in. They cannot be kept out; after long struggle, the masses simply change one symbol for another. The Mahommedan who thinks that every ritual, every form, image or ceremony, used by a non-Mahommedan is sinful, does not think so when he comes to his own temple the Kaba. Every religious Mahommedan whenever he prays, must imagine that he is standing in the temple of Kaba, and when he makes a pilgrimage there, there is a black stone in the wall which he must kiss, and all the kisses that have been printed on that stone by millions and millions of pilgrims, will stand up as witnesses for the benefit of the faithful, at the last day of judgment. Then there is the well of Zimzim. Mahommedans believe that the sins of whomsoever draws a little water out of that well, will be pardoned, and he will have a fresh body, and live for ever after the day of resurrection.

In others we find that the symbology comes in ths form of buildings. Protestants hold that churches are more sacred than other places. This church, as it is, stands for a sybmol. Or there is the Book. The idea of the Book, to them, is much holier than any other symbol. The image of the Cross with the Protestants, takes the place of the image of the Saint with the Catholics. It is vain to preach against the use of symbols, and why should we preach against them? There is no reason under the sun why man should not use these symbols. They have in order to represent the thing signified behind them. This universe is a symbol in and through which we are trying to grasp the thing signified, which is beyond and behind. This is the lower human constitution, and we are bound to have it so. Yet at the same time it is true that we are struggling to get to the thing signified, to get beyond the material, to the spiritual; the spirit is the goal, and not matter. Forms, images, bells, candles, books, churches temples, and all holy symbols, are very good, very helpful to the growing plant of spirituality, but thus far and no farther. In the vast majority of cases we find that the plant does not grow. It is very good to be born in a church, but it is very bad to die in a church. It is very good to be born within the limits of certain forms that help the little plant of spirituality, but if a man dies within the bonds of these forms, it shows that he has not grown, that there has been no development of the soul.

If, therefore, anyone says that symbols and rituals, and forms are to be kept for ever, that man is wrong, but if he says that these symbols and rituals are a help to the growth of the soul, when it is low and very concrete, he is right. By the way, you must not mistake this development of the soul as meaning anything intellectual. A man can be of gigantic intellect, yet spiritually he may be a baby, or even much worse than that. You can test it this moment. All of you who have been taught to believe in an Omnipresent God. Try to think of it. How few of you can have any idea of what omnipresence means? If you struggle hard you will get the idea of the ocean, if you have seen that, or the sky, or a vast stretch of green earth, or a desert if you have seen that. All these are material images, and so long as you cannot conceive of abstract *as* abstract, of the ideal *as* the ideal, you will have to grapple through these forms these material images, either inside or outside the brain, it matters not. You are all born idolaters, and idolarty is good, because it is in the constitution of human nature. Who can go beyond it? Only the perfect men, the God-men. The rest are all idolaters. So long as you see this universe before you with its forms and shapes, you are all idolaters. Do you get shapes in the brain? You get just a little sensation somewhere in the brain. Why do you imagine this universe with all these colours and forms and shapes, this immense symbolical universe? This is a gigantic idol you are worshipping. He who says he is the body, is a born idolater. You are all spirits, spirits that have no form or shape, spirits that are infinite and not matter. Therefore, anyone who thinks of himself as the body, as material, who cannot grasp the abstract, cannot think of himself as he is, except in and through matter, and is therefore an idolater. And yet how these people begin to fight with each other, each calling the other idolater; that is to say, each says his idol is all right, and the other's is all wrong.

Therefore, we will get out of these silly notions of spiritual babies, we will get beyond the prattle of men, who think that religion is merely a mass of frothy words, to whom religion is only a system of doctrines, to whom religion is only a little intellectual assent, or dissent, to whom religion is believing in certain words which their own priests tell them, to whom religion is something which their forefathers believed, to whom religion is a certain form of ideas and superstitions, to which they hold on because they are their national superstitions. We will get beyond all these and look at humanity as one vast organism slowly coming towards light, this wonderful plant, slowly unfolding itself to that wonderful truth which is called God, and the first gyrations, the first motions, towards this, are always through matter, through ritual. We cannot help it.

In the heart of all these ritualisms there stands one idea, prominent above all the rest—worship of a name. Those of you who have studied the older forms of Christianity, those of you who have studied the other religions of the world, perhaps, have remarked that there is a peculiar idea with them all, the worship of name. A name is said to be very sacred. "In the name of the Lord." You read that, among the Hebrews, the holy name was considered so holy that it could not be pronounced by an ordinary man; it was sacred beyond compare, holy beyond everything. It was the holiest of all names, and all of them thought that this very name was God. That is also true; for what is this universe but name and form? Can you think without words? Word and thought are inseparable. Try if anyone of you can separate them. Whenever you think, you are doing so through word forms. Words are the inner part, and thought is the outer part; and they must come together, they cannot be separated. The one brings the other, thought brings the word, and the word brings the thought. Thus the whole universe is, as it were, the external symbol, and behind that stands the grand name of God. Each particular body is a form, and behind that particular body is its name. As soon as you think of your friend So-and-so, there comes the idea of his body, and as soon as you think of your friend's body, you get the idea of his name. This is in the constitution of man. That is to say, psychologically, in the mind-stuff of man there cannot come the idea of name without the idea of form, and there cannot come the idea of form without the idea of name. They are inseparable; they are the external and the internal sides of the same wave. As such, names have been exalted and worshipped all over the world, consciously or unconsciously man found the glory of names.

Again, we find that, in many different religions, holy personages have been worshipped. They worship Krishna, they worship Buddha, they worship Jesus, and so forth. Then there is the worship of saints; hundreds of them have been worshipped all over the world, why not? The vibration of light is everywhere. The owl sees in the dark. That shows it is there. But man cannot see it there. For the man, that vibration is only visible in the lamp, in the sun, in the moon. God is omnipresent; He is manifesting Himself in every being, but for men He is only visible, recognisable in man. When His light, His presence, His spirit, shines through the human face divine, then, and then alone, can man understand Him. Thus man has been worshipping God through men all the time, and must so worship Him as long as he remains man. He may cry against it, struggle against it, but as soon as he attempts to realise God, he will find the constitutional necessity of thinking of God as a man. So we find that these are the three primary points which we have in the worship of God, in almost every religion—forms or symbols, names, God-men. All religions have these, but then you find that they want to fight with each other. One says "My name is the only name, and not yours, and my form is the only form, and not yours, and my God-men are the only God-men in the world, and yours are simply myths." In modern times the Christian clergymen have become a little kinder; so they say that in all these older religions the different forms of worship were foreshadowings of what was going to happen; which, of course, is the only true form—their own. God tested Himself in older times; tested His powers, by getting these things in shape, but He really worked them out in Christianity, later on. That, at least, is a good step in advance of the old position. Fifty years ago they would not have said even that; everything was ignored except their own religion, and that was everything. This idea is not limited to any religion, or any nation, or any state of persons; people are always thinking that the only thing to be done is what they themselves do, and that is where the study of different religions helps us. It shows us that the same thoughts that we have been calling ours, and ours alone, were present hundreds of years ago in others, and sometimes even in a better form of expression than our own.

These are the external forms of devotion, through which man has to pass, but if he is sincere, if he really wants to reach the truth, he gets higher than these, to a plane where forms are as nothing. Forms are simply the kindergarten of religion, the child's preparation. Temples or churches, books or forms, are just for the child's play, so as to make the spiritual man strong enough to take yet higher steps, and these first steps are necessary to be taken if he wants religion. With that thirst, that want for God, comes real devotion, real *Bhakti*. Who wants? That is the question. Religion is not doctrines, nor dogmas, nor intellectual argumentation; it is being and becoming; it is realisation. We hear everybody talking about God and soul, and all the mysteries of the universe, but if you will take them one by one, and ask them "Have you realised God? Have you seen your Soul?" How many dare say they have? And yet they are all fighting! Once in India, representatives of different sects got together, and began to dispute. One said that the only God was Shiva; another said the only God was Vishnu, and so on, and there was no end to their discussions. A sage was passing that way, and he was invited by the disputants to join with them. He went there, and the first question he asked was of the man who was claiming Shiva as the greatest God; "Have you seen Shiva? Are you acquainted with him? If not, how do you know He is the greatest God?" He asked the same question of the other party; "Have you seen Vishnu?" And after asking this question of all of them it was found out that not one of them had known anything of God; and that was why they were disputing so much; had they really known, they would not have been disputing. When a jar is being filled it makes all sorts of noises, but when it is full it is calm and silent; it has known the truth, So the very fact of these disputations and fightings among sects shows that they do not know anything about religion; religion to them is a mere mass of frothy words, to be written in books. Each one hurries to write a big book, to make it as massive as possible, to steal from everybody he can lays his hands on, and never acknowledges his indebtedness, and then he wants to launch this book on the world, to make one more disturbance in these already existing hundred thousand fights.

The vast majority of men are atheists, I am glad that, in modern times, another set of atheists has come up in the Western world, the materialists, because they are *sincere* atheists; they are better than these religious atheists, who are insincere, who *talk* about religion, and *fight* about it, and yet never *want* it, never try to *realise* it never try to *understand* it. Remember those words of Christ, "Ask and ye shall receive, seek and ye shall find, knock and it shall be opened unto you." Those words are literally true, not figures, or fictions. They were ground out of the heart's blood of one of the greatest children of God who ever came to this world of ours, words which came as the fruit of realisation, not from books, but from a man who had realised God Himself, and had felt God; who had spoken with God, lived with God, a hundred times more intensely than you or I see this building. Who wants God? That is the question. Do you think all this mass of people in the world want God, and cannot get Him? That cannot be. What want is there without its external object? Do you ever see men wanting to breathe and there is no such thing as air for them to breathe? Did you ever hear of a man who wanted to eat, and there was no such thing as food? What creates these desires? The existence of external things. It was the light that made the eyes; it was the sound that made the ears. So every desire in human beings has been created by something which already existed outside, and this desire for perfection, for reaching the goal, and getting beyond nature, how can it be there, until something has drilled it into the soul of man, created it, and made it live there? He, therefore, in whom this desire is awakened, will reach the goal. But who wants? We want everything but God. This is not religion that you see all around you. My lady has varieties of furniture, from all over the world, in her parlour, but now it is the fashion to have a Japanese something, and she buys a vase, and puts it in some corner. Such is religion with the vast majority; they have all sorts of things for enjoyment, and without just a little flavour of religion, life is not all right, because society would criticise. Society says something; so, he or she has some religion. This is the present state of religion in the world.

A disciple went to his master and said to him, "Sir, I want religion." The master looked at the young man, and did not speak; only smiled. The young man came every day, and insisted that he wanted religion. But the old man knew better than the young man. One day, when it was very hot, he asked the young man to go to the river with him, and take a plunge. The young man plunged in, and the old man after him, and held the young man down under the water by main force. When the young man had struggled for a good while, the old man let him rise, and said, "What did you want most whilst you were under the water?" "A breath of air," the disciple answered. "Do you want God that way? If you do, you will get Him in a moment." Until you have that thirst, that desire, you cannot get religion, however you struggle with your intellect, or your books, or your forms. Until that thirst is awakened in you, you are no better than any atheist, only that the atheist is sincere, and you are not.

A great sage used to say, "Suppose there is a thief in a room, and somehow he gets to know that there is a vast mass of gold in the next room, and there is only a thin partition between the two rooms, what would be the condition of that thief? He would be sleepless, he would not be able to eat, or do anything. His whole mind would be on that gold. How to drill a hole in that wall, and get at the wealth, would be his whole thought; and do you mean to say that if all these people really believed that the mine of happiness, of blessedness, of Glory, God Himself, were here, they would again go and do just as usual in the world, without trying to get God?" As soon as a man begins to believe there is a God, he becomes mad with longing to get to Him. Others may go their way, but as soon as a man is sure that there is a much higher life than that which he is leading here, as soon as he feels sure that the senses are not all, that this limited, material body is as nothing compared with the immortal, eternal, undying bliss of the Self, he becomes mad until he finds this bliss out for himself, and this madness, this thirst, this mania, is what is called the "awakening" to religion, and when that has come, a man is beginning to be religious. But it takes a long time. All these forms and ceremonies, these prayers, and pilgrimages, these books, bells, candles, and priests, are the preparations; they take off the impurities from the soul; and when the soul has become pure, it naturally wants to get to its own source, the mine of all purity, God Himself. Just as a piece of iron, which had been covered with the dust of centuries, though it was lying near a huge magnet all the time, is weighed down, when by some cause or other this dust is cleared off, its natural attraction manifests, and the iron is drawn towards the magnet. So, this human soul, covered with the dust of ages, impurities, wickedness, and sins, after millions of births, by these forms and ceremonies, by doing good to others, loving other beings, becomes purified, and when it is purified enough, its natural attractions come, and it wakens up, and struggles towards God. This is the beginning of religion.

Yet, all these forms and symbols are simply the beginning; not love proper. Love we hear spoken of everywhere. Every one says love God,

Men do not know what it is to love ; if they did, they would not talk so lightly about it. Every man says he can love, and then, in five minutes, finds out there was no love in his nature. Every woman says she can love, and finds out in three minutes that she cannot. The world is full of talk of love, but it is hard to love. Where is love ? How do you know that there is love ? The first test of love is that it knows no bargain. So long as you see a man love another to get something, you may know that it is not love ; it is shopkeeper's love. Wherever there is any question of buying or selling, it is no more love. So, when any man is praying to God "give me this and give me that," it is not love. How can it be ? I give you my little prayer, and you give me something in return ; that is what it is, mere shopkeeping.

There was a certain great king who went to hunt in a forest, and there he happened to meet a sage. He had a little conversation with this sage, and became so pleased with him that he asked him to accept a present from him. "No," said the sage, "I am perfectly satisfied with my condition ; these trees give me enough fruits to eat ; these beautiful pure streams supply me with all the water I want : I sleep in these caves. What do I care for your presents, though you be an emperor." The emperor said : "Just to purify myself, to gratify me, take some present, and come with me into the city." At last the sage consented to go with this emperor, and he was brought into the emperor's palace, wherein were gold, and jewellery, and marble, and most wonderful things. Wealth and power were manifest in this palace, and there that poor sage from the forest was ushered in. The emperor asked him to wait a minute while he repeated his prayer, and he went into a corner and began to pray, "Lord, give me more wealth, more children, more territory." In the meanwhile the sage got up, and began to walk away. The emperor saw him going, and went after him. "Stay, sir, you did not take my present, and are going away." The sage turned round to him and said: "Beggar, I do not beg of beggars. What have been begging yourself all the time." That is not the language of love. What is the difference between love and shopkeeping, if you ask God to give you this, and give you that? The first test of love is that it knows no bargaining; it always gives. Love takes upon itself the stand of a giver, and never that of a taker. Says the child of God: "If God wants, I give him even my threadbare coat, but I do not want anything of Him, I want nothing in this univese. I love Him because I want to love Him, and I ask no favour in return. Who cares whether God is almighty or not, because I do not want any power from Him, nor any manifestation of His power. Sufficient for me that He is the God of love. I ask no more questions."

The second test is that love knows no fear. How can you frighten love? Does the lamb love the lion? The mouse the cat? The slave the master? Slaves sometimes simulate love, but is it love? Where do you ever see love in fear? It is always sham. So long as man thinks of God as sitting above the clouds, with a reward in one hand, and punishment in the other, there can be no love. With love never comes the idea of fear, or of anything that makes us afraid. Think of a young mother in the street and a dog barking at her; she flies into the next house. Suppose the next day she is in the street with her child and a lion is upon the child; where will be her position? Just in the mouth of the lion, protecting her child. Love conquers all fear. So also is love to God. Who cares whether God is a rewarder or a punisher? That is not the thought of a lover. Think of a judge, when he comes home, what does his wife see in him? Not a judge, or a rewarder, or a punisher, but her husband, her lover. What do the children see in him? Their loving father, not the punisher or rewarder. So the children of God never see in Him a punisher or rewader. It is all outside people, who have never tasted love, begin to fear, and quake away their lives. Cast off all fear—these are horrible ideas of God as a punisher or rewarder, though they may have their use in savage minds. Some men, even the most intellectual, are spiritual savages, and these ideas may help them. But to men who are spiritual, men who are approaching religion, in whom spiritual insight is awakened, such ideas are simply childish, simply foolish. Such men reject all ideas of fear.

The third is still a higher test. Love is always the highest ideal. When one has passed through the first two stages—when he has thrown off all shop-keeping, and cast off all fear—he then begins to realise that love was always the highest ideal. How many times in this world we see that the most beautiful woman loves the ugliest men. How many times we see one of the handsomest of men love a very ugly woman. Where is the attraction to them? Those that are standing aside see the ugly man, or the ugly woman, but not the lover, to the lover they are the most beautiful beings that ever existed. How is it? The woman who was loving the ugly man took, as it were, the ideal of beauty which was in her own brain, and projected it over this ugly man, and what she worshipped and loved was, not the ugly man, but her own ideal. That man, was, as it were, only the suggestion, and upon that suggestion she threw her own ideal, and covered it, and it became her object of worship. Now this applies in every case where we love. Think how many of us have very common looking brothers or sisters, yet the very idea of brother makes them to us the handsomest of men, and the very idea of sister makes them the handsomest of women.

The philosophy in the background is that each one projects his ideal and worships that. This external world is only the world of suggestion. All that we see, we project out of our own minds. A grain of sand gets into the shell of an oyster. It begins to irritate the oyster, and the oyster immediately covers the sand with a secretion of its own juice, and the result is the beautiful pearl. This is what we are all doing. External things are only the bits of sand which are making the suggestions, and over these we project our own ideals, and cover the externals. The wicked will see this world as a perfect hell, and the good will see it as a perfect heaven. Lovers see this world as full of love, and haters as full of hatred, fighters see nothing but fighting in the world, peacemakers nothing but peace, the perfect man sees nothing but God. So we always worship our highest ideal, and when we have reached the point when we love the ideal, *as* the ideal, all arguments and doubts have vanished for ever. Who cares whether a God can be demonstrated or not? The ideal can never escape, because it is a part of my own nature. I shall only question that ideal, when I question my own existence, and as I cannot question the one, I shall not question the other. Who cares whether science can demonstrate to me a God outside of myself, living somewhere, managing this universe by fits and starts, creating it for several days, and then going to sleep for the rest of time? Who cares whether God can be Almighty, and all Merciful, at the same time, or not? Who cares whether He is the rewarder of mankind, whether He looks at us with the eyes of a tyrant, or with the eyes of a beneficent monarch? The lover has passed beyond all these things, beyond rewards and punishments, beyond fears, or doubts, or scientific, or any other demonstration. Sufficient unto him is the ideal of love, and is it not self-evident that this universe is but a manifestation of this love. What is it that makes atoms come and join atoms, molecule, molecule, sets big planets flying towards each other, attracts man to woman, woman to man, human beings to human beings, animals to animals, drawing the whole universe, as it were, towards one centre? This is what is called love. Its manifestation is from the lowest atom to the highest ideal, omnipresent, all-pervading, everywhere is this love. What is manifesting itself as attraction in sentient and insentient, in the particular and in the universal, is the love of God. It is the one motive power that is in the universe. Under the impetus of that love, Christ stands to give up His life for humanity, Buddha for an animal, the mother for the child, the father for the wife. It is under the impetus of the same love that men are ready to give up their lives for their country, and strange to say, under the impetus of that same love, the thief goes to steal, the murderer to murder; for even in these cases, the spirit is the same, but the manifestation is different. This is the one motive power in the universe. The thief had love for gold, the love was there but it was misdirected. So, in all crimes, as well as in all virtuous actions, behind stands that eternal love. Suppose one of you takes out a piece of paper from your pocket, and writes a cheque for a thousand dollars for the poor of New York, and at the same time I take a piece of paper, and I try to forge your name. The light will be the same for both; you and I are responsible for the manifestation, it is not light that is to blame. Unattached, yet shining in everything, the motive power of the universe, without which the universe will fall to pieces in a moment, is love, and this love is God.

"None, O beloved, loves the husband for the husband's sake, but for the Self* that is in the husband she loves the husband; none O beloved, ever loves the wife for the wife's sake, but for the Self that is in the wife. None ever loved anything else, except for the Self." Even this selfishness, which is so much condemned, is but a manifestation of the same love. Stand aside from this play, do not mix in it, but see this wonderful panorama, this grand drama, played scene after scene, hear this wonderful harmony; all are the one manifestation of the same love. Even in selfishness, that Self will multiply, grow and grow. That one Self, the one man, will become two selves when he gets married, several, when he gets children, will become a whole village, a whole city, and yet grow and grow until he will take the whole world as his Self, the whole universe as his Self. That Self, in the long run, will gather all men, all women, all children, all animals, the whole universe. It will have

*The Eternal Self (*Atman*) which is the Efficient and Material Cause of the World.

grown into one mass of universal love, infinite love, and that love is God.

Thus we come to what is called supreme *Bhakti*, surpreme devotion, when forms and symbols have fallen off. One who has reached that cannot enter into any sect, for all sects are in him. What shall he enter? Such a one cannot enter into any temple or church, for all churches and temples are in him. Where is the church big enough for him? Such a one cannot bind himself down to certain limited forms. Where is the limit for Unlimited Love, with which he has become one? In all religions which take up this ideal of love we find the struggle to express it. Although we understand what this love means, and though we see that everything in this world of affections and attractions is but a manifestation, partial or otherwise, of that Infinite love, the exprssion which has been attempted by sages aud saints of different nations, yet we find them ransacking the powers of language until the most carnal expressions stand transfigured.

Thus sang the Royal Hebrew sage, thus sang they of India. "O beloved, one kiss of Thy lips, one that has been kissed by Thee, his thirst for Thee increaseth for ever. All sorrows cease, and he forgets the past, present and future, and only thinks of Thee alone." That is the madness of the lover, when all desires have vanished. Who cares for salvation? Who cares to be saved? Who cares to be perfect even? Who cares for freedom? says the lover.

I do not want wealth, no, not even health, I do not want beauty, do not want intellect; let me be born again and again, amid all the evils that are in the world; I will not complain, but let me love Thee, and that for love's sake. That is the madness of love, which finds its expression in these songs, and the highest, most expressive, strongest, the most attractive human love is that between the sexes, and it was therefore that language which they took up. It was the madness of sexual love that was the faintest echo of the mad love of the saint. These are they who want to become mad, inebriated with the love of God; "God intoxicated men." They want to drink the cup of love which has been brewed by saints and sages of every religion, in which those great lovers of God have poured their hearts' blood, into which have been concentrated all the hopes of those who have loved without seeking reward, who wanted love itself. They wanted nothing beyond love; the reward of love is love, and what a reward it is! It is the only thing that takes off all sorrows, the only cup by the drinking of which this disease of the world vanishes. Man becomes divinely mad, and forgets that he is man.

Lastly, we find that all these various systems, in the end, converge to that one point, that perfect union. We always begin as dualists. God is a separate being and I am a separate being. Love comes in the middle, and man begins to approach God, and God, as it were, begins to approach man. Man takes up all the various relationships of life, as father, as mother, as friend, as lover ; he exists as all these, and the last point comes when he becomes one with the object of worship, that I am you, and you are that I, and worshipping you, I worship myself, and in worshipping myself, I worship you. There we find the highest explanation of that with which man begins. Where we begin, there we end. At the beginning it was love for the Self, but the claims of the little self made love selfish ; at the end came the full blaze of light, when that Self had become the Infinite. That God, who, at first, was a body somewhere, became resolved, as it were, into Infinite Love. Man himself was also transformed. He was approaching God, he was throwing off all vain desires of which he was full before. With desires vanished selfishness, and at the apex, he found that Love, Lover, and Beloved are One.